"Among the various arguments for the existence of God through the centuries, perhaps the most neglected and unknown is the argument from human desire. . . . Puckett presents the salient elements of the argument and engages the key contributors and critics. He does so with a fervency and deftness that serves to re-present this important argument for the existence of God to our age."

—MICHAEL R. YOUNG

co-editor of *The Journal of Faith and the Academy*

"C. S. Lewis . . . argues that the best explanation for the human experience of joy and the accompanying longing for the transcendent and permanent is found in the Judeo-Christian creation narrative. . . . Until now, Lewis's interesting argument has largely been neglected by apologists making a case for Christian theism. But I believe the argument from desire has a rightful place within a comprehensive, cumulative-case argument for theism, and I am delighted that Joe Puckett's The Apologetics of Joy fills this gap by developing the argument and defending it against its detractors. The Apologetics of Joy is, to my knowledge, the first book-length treatment on Lewis's argument, and I am happy to commend it to its readers."

—MARK LINVILLE

contributor to *The Blackwell Companion to Natural Theology* and coauthor and coeditor of *Philosophy and the Christian Worldview*

The Apologetics of Joy

The Apologetics of Joy

A Case for the Existence of God
from C. S. Lewis's Argument from Desire

Joe Puckett Jr.

Foreword by Mark Linville

WIPF & STOCK · Eugene, Oregon

THE APOLOGETICS OF JOY
A Case for the Existence of God from C. S. Lewis's Argument from Desire

Copyright © 2012 Joe Puckett Jr. All rights reserved. Except for brief quotations in critical publications or reviews, no part of this book may be reproduced in any manner without prior written permission from the publisher. Write: Permissions, Wipf and Stock Publishers, 199 W. 8th Ave., Suite 3, Eugene, OR 97401.

Wipf & Stock
An Imprint of Wipf and Stock Publishers
199 W. 8th Ave., Suite 3
Eugene, OR 97401
www.wipfandstock.com

ISBN 13: 978-1-62032-373-1
Manufactured in the U.S.A.

All scripture quotations, unless otherwise indicated, are taken from the Holy Bible, New International Version®, NIV®. Copyright ©1973, 1978, 1984 by Biblica, Inc.™ Used by permission of Zondervan. All rights reserved worldwide.

All Scriptures taken from the New King James Version. Copyright © 1982 by Thomas Nelson, Inc. Used by permission. All rights reserved

To my wife Stefani:

Who teaches me love and more, always more.

"The homemaker has the ultimate career. All other careers exist for one purpose only—and that is to support the ultimate career." —C. S. Lewis

To Faith and Hope:

Two creative daughters who teach me everything their names imply and always remind me to use my imagination.

"A children's story that can only be enjoyed by children is not a good children's story in the slightest." —C. S. Lewis

And

To Dr. Mark Linville:

A Christian analytical philosopher who has made my brain hurt many times from thinking too much. Thanks for being such a great friend and mentor.

"We read to know that we are not alone" —C. S. Lewis

Contents

Foreword xi
Preface xiii
Introduction xvii

PART 1   C. S. LEWIS AND THE ARGUMENT FROM DESIRE   1

1   The Argument as Presented in Selected Works of C. S. Lewis   13
2   Defining "Joy" as *Sehnsucht*   22
3   Plantinga and Lewis: Balancing the Mystical
      and the Natural in *Sehnsucht*   28
4   A Word on the Different Forms that the Argument Can Take   35

**PART 2   EXAMINING BEVERSLUIS'S OBJECTIONS
              TO THE ARGUMENT   43**

5   Does Lewis "Beg the Question"?   47
6   Does the Quality of *Sehnsucht* Lack Innateness?   52
7   If "Joy" Is So Natural and Desirable Then Why Did Lewis
      Run Away from It?   56
8   Does the Concept of *Sehnsucht* Contradict the Bible?   61
9   Why Do Some People Never Experience
      what C. S. Lewis Calls "Joy"?   66

PART 3   HAUNTED BY DESIRE   77

10   Echoes and Evidences of the Second Premise   81
11   Imagination and the Heart's Deep Need for a Happy Ending   86
12   In the Defense of Beauty   98
13   Lewis, Leisure, and *Sehnsucht*   110

PART 4   CONCERNING THE CONCLUSION OF THE ARGUMENT
         FROM DESIRE   119

14   The Evolutionary Objection   123
15   Is there a Human Gene for *Sehnsucht*?   133

Conclusion   141
Appendix: The End of Human Desire   146
Bibliography   151
Subject/Name Index   155

Foreword

NIETZSCHE REMARKED THAT OF all the animals man is the one that has "most dangerously strayed from its instincts." He had a full range of uniquely human propensities in mind, but among these is the widespread impulse to believe in realities that transcend the natural world. Nearly nine out of every ten people living harbor some variety of religious belief. Though the beliefs themselves differ widely, a common thread is the conviction of some metaphysically and axiologically ultimate reality that infuses human existence with meaning and determines the nature and course of the human Good Life. This is a feature of human nature that calls for explanation. One sort of explanation finds the source of this widespread religious impulse in certain naturally occurring human propensities, and thus seeks to undercut both the religious beliefs and whatever experiences have spawned them. Thus, Daniel Dennett has recently suggested that the religion "meme" is a kind of self-replicating mental parasite that has infested the human mind not wholly unlike the way liver flukes infest the brains of ants. Fluke-infested ants do crazy things like climb to the tips of the grass where they are readily eaten by grazing cattle and sheep who become the new and unwitting hosts of these parasites. Humans infested with the religion meme sometimes (and sometimes do not) exhibit similarly bizarre—and sometimes self-destructive—behaviors, such as climbing atop pillars to sit in meditation for decades, or choosing to be raised up on crosses over denying their faith. Of course, if we begin with the assumption that "We exist as material beings in a material world, all of whose phenomena are the consequences of physical relations among material entities," as Richard Lewontin once dogmatically insisted, that is, if we assume the truth of naturalism, then *some* such undercutting explanation of religious belief is correct. Lewontin, of course, is determined to prevent any "divine foot" from gaining entrance to the world.

xi

Foreword

But whether anything like naturalism is true is a part of the question at hand. Another possibility is that so many of us believe in some sort of religious reality because some such thing is there to be perceived—even if only through a glass and darkly. Augustine confessed, "You have made us for Yourself, and our hearts are restless until they rest in You." He would have us believe that there is a longing in the human heart, and that longing points to an object that alone can satisfy it, namely, the very Creator who has placed eternity in our hearts. If Bertrand Russell thought it a "strange mystery" that nature, "in her secular hurryings," should have "brought forth at last a child, subject still to her power, but gifted with sight, with knowledge of good and evil, with the capacity of judging all the works of his unthinking Mother," it is stranger still that the child should have strayed from his instincts and found himself in need of things that cannot be afforded by that mother.

C. S. Lewis's "Argument from Desire" takes its cue from such observations. Lewis argues that the best explanation for the human experience of "joy" and the accompanying longing for the transcendent and permanent is found in the Judeo-Christian creation narrative. Theism explains—where naturalism explains *away*—this nearly universal feature of human nature.

Until now, Lewis's interesting argument has largely been neglected by apologists making a case for Christian theism. But I believe the Argument from Desire has a rightful place within a comprehensive "cumulative case" argument for theism, and I am delighted that Joe Puckett's *The Apologetics of Joy* fills this gap by developing the argument and defending it against its detractors. *The Apologetics of Joy* is, to my knowledge, the first book-length treatment of Lewis's argument, and I am happy to commend it to his readers.

Mark D. Linville
Fayetteville, Georgia
May 31, 2012

Preface

In his essay "Christian Apologetics," C. S. Lewis once commented, "I am to talk about Apologetics. Apologetics means of course Defense. The first question is—what do you propose to defend? Christianity of course . . ." Similarly, "God exists" is a proposition this book seeks to defend. But in the end, I hope you find out not only that there is a God, but that there is a wonderful world he has created, and that you have been given a life that is meant to be enjoyed with him. There is something about human nature that longs for this life of happiness and meaning. Thus, the good news is that there is a way to have what your heart already naturally seeks.

Consequently this book is written with three different kinds of readers in mind. It is a book for *thinking Christians* who want to know more about the nature of their faith. It is book which tries to show how faith is both an instinctive response to human nature as well as a seed divinely planted. It is the conviction of the author that this seed can (along with God's special revelation found in the Bible) grow into a life filled with something more wonderful than anything this world has to offer in its current state.

This book is also for all *thinking seekers* who want to know why they may struggle to believe. It is my hope that the contents of this book will help students of literature and/or religion, who are sincerely sitting on the fence of doubt and uncertainty, to take their first real step of faith.

But this book is also written for *C. S. Lewis readers* who simply want to learn more about a subject that was very important to him. It can well be argued that the "Argument from Desire" can be found in some form in the vast majority of Lewis's works of fiction and non-fiction.

Lewis believed that humans have a natural (albeit strangely elusive and mysterious) desire for a transcendent world. Consequently, it is a desire that nothing *on earth* can satisfy. We will get into this more later. But for now I want you to know what to expect from this book. It is a bit academic at times. But there is a reason for this. I wish to challenge your thinking. I want to show you that nothing I say in this book is completely new and has been said by thinkers long past. God's existence has been felt and perceived since the beginning of human history. While we focus on the thoughts of C. S. Lewis in this book, we will discuss many more authors, philosophers, and poets along the way. This will make this book both intellectually challenging as well as (we hope) stimulating. I write this book with both the average (but serious) reader in mind as well as the scholar who has an interest in the world of philosophy, literature, and apologetics. I seek to put together as much literary and sociological evidence as possible in a short space. While it will have been helpful for the reader to have read some of the works by C. S. Lewis before reading this book, it is not necessary. In fact, I hope this book will encourage the reader to pick up more of Lewis's works after having read this one.

The purpose for writing this book is to challenge the skeptical trend (sometimes referred to as the "New Atheism") of putting out books that seek to make believing in God look silly. But belief in God is anything but silly. Belief in the divine is ingrained in the history of human thought and experience and has inspired wonderful works of art, literature, and charity. Those who believe can see the beauty in the world in a way that the unbeliever cannot. The believer sees the universe as a divine act of creation. The unbeliever can see the beauty of the world but chooses to ignore the Artist who made it so beautiful for us to be here to see in the first place. But, as we will seek to show, in order to do this, the unbeliever must put aside his/her instincts. He/she must ignore what is most natural to the human being—the natural instinct to believe in the divine.

There have been a flood of recent books that have come out seeking to place doubt in people's minds about the existence and nature of God. And yet people continue to believe regardless of these constant challenges. There is a good reason for this. Human beings are brought into this world with a planted seed that sprouts a desire for ultimate meaning and happiness that just will not go away. It is as though something (or someone?) put those desires there. Some have sought to explain away these desires by saying that evolution (through natural selection) has allowed these thoughts to continue only for survival purposes. We talk about this theory a lot in chapters 14 and 15. But for now, I will only say that this answer is far too simplistic.

But sometimes we can't exactly explain *why* we believe. And that's okay. I cannot exactly explain why I get hungry, I just do. And when I get hungry, I eat. Faith can work this way. There are many good arguments for God's existence. But sometimes people have a hard time putting their finger on exactly *why* they believe. My proposal (which was C. S. Lewis's proposal) is that you don't always have to put your finger on it *exactly*. Belief in God springs from a natural desire like hunger. You don't have to over analyze hunger to know when you need to eat. So do not get frustrated when a skeptical book comes out trying to explain away your hunger for God. You know yourself when you are hungry. All you have to do is eat. Once you take in this divine nourishment, your life will never be the same again.

In part 1 we will discuss what C. S. Lewis said about the argument from desire. We will try to explain and define some key terms and concepts that will help you understand this argument. In part 2 we look at some objections to the argument that have been promoted by the agnostic writer John Beversluis. In part 3 we will examine some experiences of life (i.e., evidence that is *a posteriori*) that further push our natural longing (i.e., that which is *a priori*) for God along in life. In part 4 we consider one of the most important objections not considered by Beversluis—the evolutionary objection. In the conclusion we will apply all that has been said to see if the argument works and what it actually does and does not tell us about God's existence. I have added an appendix to discuss some other theological implications of the argument. In it we will discuss the ultimate goal and object of this intense longing humans have. Even though it is an appendix, in some ways, it can be thought of as making one of the most important points of the book.

I want to thank a number of people for their contribution to this work. I want to thank Paul Copan, Mike Young, and Dan Primozic for all of their helpful suggestions and insights. I also want to thank Mark Linville (one person I have dedicated this book to) for being such a great friend and mentor. He has not only taught me a lot of philosophy, but he has instilled in me the desire to be a better analytical philosopher who can more effectively learn to love the Lord my God "with all my mind" (Matt 22:37). Finally, I want to thank my wife and daughters for their enduring support and love. Without them, I could not have done this work. They are the best images on earth that help me to see what love in heaven will actually be like.

Joe Puckett Jr.
Sterling, IL
June 13, 2012

Introduction

IN HIS ESSAY *The Myth of Sisyphus*, the existentialist philosopher Albert Camus set out to demonstrate the absurdity of life. He held that all human beings longed for meaning in a world that offered none. He posed the question,

> What, then, is that incalculable feeling that deprives the mind of the sleep necessary to life? A world that can be explained even with bad reasons is a familiar world. But, on the other hand, in a universe suddenly divested of illusions and lights, man feels an alien, a stranger. His exile is without remedy since he is deprived of the memory of a lost home or the hope of a promised land. This divorce between man and his life, the actor and his setting, is properly the feeling of absurdity.[1]

Camus knew, of course, that there was nothing absurd about having a desire for meaning. Such a desire is unavoidable. Neither did he think there was anything absurd about living in a world that offered no meaning to us. For Camus, the absurdity was found in the combination of the two conflicting realities. To Camus, it was as though we live in a foodless world of starving people. In other words, mankind's problem is that he finds himself with an intense longing to hear from a mute planet. In Camus's universe, humanity is alone in this conscious search. The only sounds a person is able to hear are the echoes coming from his/her own cries for meaning bouncing off the empty space of the universe. The question now, Camus suggests, is what we will do about it. The extreme solution is suicide. Yet secular existentialists like Camus would rather humans create their own meaning in order to find whatever scraps of peace they can scavenge.

But is this true? Are we really living in a world so absurd that every person must grasp at anything just to survive? Are we in a situation where

---

1. Camus, *Myth of Sisyphus*, 6.

humanity's deepest thirst for meaning can never be quenched? Are we really deprived of the "memory of a lost home"?

It appears that Camus was only partially right. We do seem to find ourselves in a world that does not completely satisfy our most intimate desires. But then, the human mind is not easy to please. It acts as a meaning vacuum sucking up everything in its path in order to find something big enough to fill the psycho-spiritual desire it contains. And it does appear, as Camus seems to be suggesting, that there is nothing in this world big enough to fill that void. The problem seems to be, to borrow the words of the ancient writer of Ecclesiastes, that "God has put eternity into our hearts" (Eccl 3:11). Thus, in all fairness to nature, the universe is not big enough, nor sufficient enough, to fill a void that has a magnitude as great as eternity.

And yet it seems that there is another side to this apparent absurdity. Maybe the clash between the seeming silence of the world and the searching heart is not meant to cause us to give up in despair. Maybe the apparent absurdity is supposed to tell us something. While not satisfying all our longings, maybe the world is not as silent as Camus thought. But if so, then what is the world (*via* human desire) trying to tell us? Perhaps there should be a closer examination of the human condition to see if there are any clues that will give us an answer to this question.

But even if the universe, by itself, is void of meaning, does this mean there is no meaning to be found at all? There is still something to be said concerning the human mind as it contemplates the reason for its own existence. The psychology of mankind with all its capabilities will never be exhausted. But what is equally impressive is the fact that the human mind finds itself inhabiting a world that is so ready to be explored by it. No matter what worldview a person has, it ought to be agreed that it seems as if the whole world was made (or evolved) just so that the conscious mind could be at work and play. While there is plenty in life that is unpleasant, and while the world may not satisfy our souls completely, if one sits quietly under the stars long enough to think, there also seems to be an undeniable sense in which the universe is still here to tell us about something more wonderful than itself. If Camus was right that the world cannot give us what we truly long for, then maybe he was looking in the wrong place. Or to say it more accurately: maybe he was looking in the right place but in the wrong way. What if Camus expected more from the universe than it was intended to give? It is as if Camus expected the universe itself to be the divine thing that gave us everything we craved. But, if such is not the case, then what exactly was Camus missing? This book will present an argument that seeks to answer this very question.

Camus's view of reality implies that the universe and the human minds that live in it are incompatible entities. But maybe the world is more beautifully designed and the mind more carefully suited for it than Camus thought. We should stop and ask why rational minds should exist to experience such a beautiful world at all? And why should there be such a beautiful world for rational minds to experience? Whatever else might be said about the relationship, it certainly appears that both earth and life were made for each other. As far as dependency goes, however, it is mainly a one-sided relationship. No matter how much humanity tries to "save" the planet, it is the planet that continues to provide all the resources that sustains humanity. The truth is, we are obviously and utterly dependent animals. While many see the divine responsibility to care for our world, there is no doubt that we are really the ones with such diverse and desperate needs. In fact, we have many needs that only a world like ours could sufficiently provide for. Abraham Maslow summarized at least five of humanity's most basic needs: physiological, safety, love/belonging, esteem, and self-actualization.[2] Others have identified more. But however many needs we have, one thing we can be absolutely sure of—where there are needs, there are desires to crave their fulfillment.

In order to guarantee that our needs be met, humans have an amazing innate capacity to desire the objects that satisfy them. Desire is what keeps people going. It motivates and moves us to act accordingly and (though not always) appropriately. Desire is a natural alarm system to tell us when something is demanding our attention.

There are many desires humans have, and there are infinite ways to fill them. Some desires are healthy for us; others are addictive and unhealthy. Some desires are natural; others are developed only by habit. Some desires are universal to the human species; others are artificial and specific to a certain way of life. Some desires have real objects that correspond to them; others fall into the category of mere wishful thinking

---

2. According to Gerrig and Zimbardo, "self-actualization" refers to the human need to reach the full "development of their potentials . . . A self-actualizing person is self-aware, self-accepting, socially responsive, creative, spontaneous and open to novelty and challenge, among other positive attributes." See Gerrig and Zimbardo, *Psychology and Life*, 388–89.

Introduction

toward non-existent objects. Some desires will be satisfied and some will not (or cannot) be.

But as wonderful as this world is, does it really provide for all of humanity's natural and universal needs? If Albert Camus was right, then there is at least one universal and natural need that is not satisfied—at least, not in this life.

Thus, the argument set forth in this book concerns whether or not mankind has a desire for a real object that corresponds to it but yet does not exist anywhere in this world (call it a desire for transcendence). We will consider how this sense of longing for transcendence is itself a gift that is intended not only to fill life with wonder and excitement, but also points us toward a yet greater joy. This desire is, in the words of C. S. Lewis, "An unsatisfied desire which is itself more desirable than any other satisfaction."[3]

Consequently, Lewis would agree with Camus that human nature universally craves an objective and transcendent meaning in life. He would also agree with Camus that the natural universe is not sufficient to satisfy every part of the human condition, including his search for ultimate meaning. But he would disagree with Camus that this apparent dilemma would mean that there was no grand meaning to be found anywhere *at all*. Thus we will explore how this unfulfilled longing for meaning and transcendence can suggest to us that something like the divine may actually exist in a place where Camus forgot to look.

But how will we do this? We will begin by looking at two representative attempts at finding the source for humanity's natural desire for the divine that comes from a naturalistic perspective: namely, attempts by Friedrich Nietzsche and Sigmund Freud. We will then turn to one of the most popular Christian philosophers (mentioned above) known for his argument for the existence of God using what is often referred to as the "Argument from Desire"—C. S. Lewis. We will discuss the substance of Lewis's argument found in his own works. Then we will turn to some objections commonly used against it. Furthermore, we will look in greater detail at the premises and see how the argument fits with the actual condition of humanity and the world he finds himself in.

---

3. Lewis, *Surprised*, 17–18.

PART 1

C. S. Lewis and the Argument from Desire

Introduction

THERE ARE MANY DIFFERENT kinds of arguments that seek to prove (or point to) the existence of a transcendent divine being. Some of these arguments are external in nature and some are internal. As the name suggests, the external arguments are those "external" to, or outside of, persons. Two kinds of external arguments are the cosmological and teleological. The cosmological argument seeks to find and explain the reason the universe exists. It tries to do so by finding either a "first cause" or a "sufficient cause" for the origin of the world and the contingent effects found within the cosmos. The difference between the two being that the first cause argument seeks to find the cause for the beginning of the universe. It assumes that the universe is finite in time. The argument from a sufficient cause does not necessarily assume the universe is finite in time but that it is still contingent in its nature. It seeks to find the non-contingent and sufficient cause of the contingent universe.[1] Aquinas is known for defending this kind of cosmological argument.[2] The teleological argument seeks to explain the apparent design of the universe. It asserts that if there is evidence of design in the world that this would imply an adequate designer to have so designed it. All arguments such as these have in common the fact that they are external to humanity's subjective or psychological being.

Internal arguments for the existence of God are different in that they lie within the very nature of humanity. This does not simply mean that it looks to the design of humanity's biological functions. Such would be associated with the teleological argument. But internal arguments seek to explain something about humanity's psychological and moral functions. One such example is the moral argument, which either explains the source of humanity's inner conscience or explains the source for objective moral laws that govern people's behaviors. In the case of the former, the

---

1. See Adler's *How to Think About God*, chapters 5, 12–14, for a fuller description of the two kinds of cosmological arguments.
2. See Aquinas, *Summa Theologiae* 1.2.3; or Kreeft, ed., *Summa*, 66–67.

argument explains how conscience got its universal authority (e.g., why do all people believe that it is wrong to violate their own conscience?). In the case of the latter, the argument states that if there is a set of universal moral laws, then there must be a universal moral lawgiver. Yet another internal argument is Victor Reppert's "Argument from Reason," which, similar to the subject of this book, is strongly tied to the work of C. S. Lewis. This argument basically affirms that a non-rational universe could not have evolved a rational mind. It holds that physical properties of the brain cannot explain the logical inferences we make *about* a proposition. We know that something is true or false, not because it exists in the world, but because we can draw conclusions *about* it. This is called *intentionality*. But where does this rational mind come from? How can an atheist claim to trust their conclusions if it is only based upon non-rational physical things like atoms in brains? The "Argument from Reason" suggests that a rational Creator is a better explanation for human rationality than a non-rational process like naturalistic evolution. As Reppert concludes in his book, "C. S. Lewis's dangerous idea is the idea that if we explain reason naturalistically we shall end up explaining it away, that is, explaining it in such a way that it cannot serve as a foundation for the natural sciences that are themselves the foundation for naturalism."[3]

The "Argument from Desire" in a Nutshell

While there are other internal arguments like Reppert's,[4] the kind that serves as the subject for this book is commonly called the "Argument

---

3. Reppert, *Dangerous Idea*, 128.

4. Another such intriguing argument comes from Alvin Plantinga's evolutionary argument against naturalism. It basically states that if our cognitive faculties that lead us to certain conclusions have evolved from naturalistic means, then there would be no way to ensure that these faculties could be reliable. There would be no way to trust conclusions that come from cognitive faculties that were designed by non-intelligent and accidental forces. Natural selection is not a mechanism that is partial to truth. It is a mechanism that simply allows a species to survive. But if we accept this as true, then the whole notion of belief in naturalism "shoots itself in the foot." For if evolutionary naturalism is true, then I could not have any way of counting on my cognitive faculties to bring me to the truth about anything. For if I cannot rely on my faculties, then I cannot rely on the conclusions that my faculties make. But if this is the case, then I cannot count on my belief that evolutionary naturalism is itself true. But if I cannot rely on this belief then I am not warranted in believing it. Thus, evolutionary naturalism would serve to undercut its own assertions. A better explanation is that something like theism must be true. For

from Desire" and is unique in many respects. While we will define the argument in greater detail below, it basically affirms that every natural and universal desire has an object that exists that satisfies that desire. Thus, if we find that humans have a natural desire for God, then there must be a God (or something like God) that exists.

This Argument from Desire is one that appeals to the human psyche. It makes no claim to being the final word on the matter of who God is. The Argument from Desire is different from many other arguments in that it appeals to the subjective first-person experience. While it presents an inductive case that all men have a desire for a transcendent (i.e., divine) reality, it nonetheless appeals to all individually to look inside their own souls to test the strength of this argument. It also calls us to look out into the world and see if we can interpret its existence in light of the argument's claims. As Peter Kreeft states, "The argument then depends on a personal appeal to introspective experience. Just as we cannot argue effectively about color with a blind man because he has no data, so we cannot argue about this desire with someone who cannot find the desire in question in himself, or who refuses to look for it, or who refuses to admit its presence once it is found."[5]

The argument holds that all people have the desire in question, though not everyone consciously identifies it as such. We, thus, believe the argument to be a rational and compelling one. But this does not mean that it is logically undeniable. McGrath says that it is not a "rigorous, logical 'proof' of God's existence; it works at a much deeper level. It may lack logical force, but it possesses existential depth. It is about the capacity of the Christian faith to address the depths of human experience—the things that really matter."[6]

Because of this point Kreeft thinks "that it is the single most intriguing argument in the history of human thought."[7]

---

since we most often believe that we *can* rely on our cognitive faculties to bring us to true conclusions, then the better explanation is to think that these faculties were designed by a cognitive faculty maker. Such a maker would itself seem to have reliable cognitive faculties of its own. Thus, theism offers a more robust account of our rational being than naturalism. See Plantinga *Where the Conflict Really Lies*, 307–50.

5. Kreeft, *Heaven*, 203
6. McGrath, *Mere Apologetics*, 112.
7. Kreeft, *Heaven*, 202

But one thing seems clear. If a person comes to accept the argument's conclusion, they will never look at the world the same way again. They will not look at *themselves* the same way again. Of all the arguments for the existence of God, we believe that this one possesses the greatest potential to change a person's life and the way they see the world around them. While there are good arguments for the existence of God that appeal to the human condition, the Argument from Desire appeals to something more specific and unique. It appeals to the human experience of longing for something more than anything this natural world has yet provided for.

Peter Kreeft states his opinion of this argument when he says that, "it is far more moving, arresting, and apologetically effective than any other argument for God or heaven."[8] Desire is something we live with every day. It is such a strong presence that we cannot help but draw attention to it. Everything from hunger, thirst, sex, friendship, and sleep fills our lives daily. The cosmological argument might only be remembered when we look at the stars on a clear night sky. The Argument from Desire can be remembered whenever we need to take a breath. We can always keep the cosmological argument at arm's length. But while cosmological and teleological arguments appeal to the head, the Argument from Desire appeals to the heart as well. This does not make it merely a "feel good" argument, for we shall see later that there is a logical case to be made from it.

Although the Argument from Desire may not, by itself, convert the masses, we believe it will serve to reaffirm or motivate the faith of those who either already believe or are sitting on the fence of uncertainty. It might not be the apologetic case to end all disputes, but it will show that belief can, in fact, be both rationally and naturally warranted. It is the contention of this author that, while the formal Argument from Desire may not convert the masses, the heart of what lies behind the argument has been what has converted most humans to religious belief. No matter what the source, there is, as will be further demonstrated below, a universal longing for the divine (or something like it). Even the agnostic psychologist Sigmund Freud stated that religious ideas are "the fulfillments of oldest, strongest, and most urgent wishes of mankind."[9]

The question that must still be asked is that, of all the desires in the world we have, why do we desire God? What is its purpose? Even looking

---

8. Ibid., 201.
9. Freud, *Future*, 30.

at it through strictly an evolutionary lens, why would natural selection favor a longing for something that has never existed? We will revisit this question in more detail in part 4.

Past Attempts to Explain Humanity's Desire for God's Existence

There have been many attempts, of course, at identifying the source for humanity's desire for God. Friedrich Nietzsche sought to explain the existence of transcendent deities by suggesting they arose as a result of immortalizing heroes such as those that exemplify the "superman" Nietzsche praised. In *The Genealogy of Morals* Nietzsche proposed that the "ancestors of the most powerful tribes are bound eventually to grow to monstrous dimensions through the imagination of growing fear and to recede into the darkness of the divinely uncanny and unimaginable: in the end the ancestor must necessarily be transformed into a god. Perhaps this is even the origin of gods, an origin therefore out of fear!"[10]

Sigmund Freud's psychoanalytic explanation offers another well-known attempt toward explaining this apparent natural desire for God. Freud suggested, similar to Nietzsche, that fear and the need for protection serves as the underlying projection of the supernatural. But, as will be explained below, Freud found the source of this need in the individual home rather than the tribal leader. Freud's theory also brought into view the role of the illusive subconscious that he believed motivated humanity's desire for religion.

When a baby first comes into the world the mother serves as the initial source for security. According to Freud's theory, the child sees the father as a threat to this mother and child relationship. Once the child comes to an age wherein he/she realizes that the father serves as a greater source for security, the relationship changes. Even though the fear of threat is still present, the child now relies on the father for safety. Once the child comes to a period wherein he/she realizes that the father will one day die, the child projects that father figure to an eternal and immortal source where that safety will forever be available. Thus, the desire for God, according to Freud, is nothing more than a subconscious illusion that gives the child/adult a false sense of security.

10. Nietzsche, *Genealogy*, 89.

The Apologetics of Joy

Even though the father serves as a source for safety, the ambivalence of the relationship continues throughout childhood. Freud explains that,

> The mother, who satisfies the child's hunger, becomes its first love-object and certainly also its first protection against all the undefined dangers which threaten it in the external world—its first protection against anxiety, we may say. In this function . . . the mother is soon replaced by the stronger father, who retains that position for the rest of childhood. But the child's attitude to its father is colored by a peculiar ambivalence. The father himself constitutes a danger for the child, perhaps because of its earlier relation to its mother. Thus it fears him no less than it longs for him and admires him. The indications of this ambivalence in the attitude to the father are deeply imprinted in every religion . . . When the growing individual finds that he is destined to remain a child forever, that he can never do without protection against strange superior powers, he lends those powers the features belonging to the figure of his father; he creates for himself the gods whom he dreads, whom he seeks to propitiate, and whom he nevertheless entrusts with his own protection.[11]

Freud put this longing for God in more blunt terms in *Civilization and its Discontents*,

> Thus we are perfectly willing to acknowledge that the "oceanic" feeling exists in many people, and we are inclined to trace it back to an early phase of ego-feeling. The further question then arises, what claim this feeling has to be regarded as the source of religious needs.
> To me the claim does not seem compelling. After all, a feeling can only be a source of energy if it is itself the expression of a strong need. The derivation of religious needs from the infant's helplessness and the longing for the father aroused by it seems to me too incontrovertible, especially since the feeling is not simply prolonged in childhood days, but is permanently sustained by fear of the superior power of Fate. I cannot think of any need in childhood as strong as the need for a father's protection.[12]

Thus, while denying that the "oceanic feeling" was the true source for "religious needs," Freud believed that the desire for God (at first felt in the child's "longing for the father") was simply the outcome of the human need for security (i.e., the "infant's helplessness"). The British scholar,

---

11. Freud, *Future*, 24.
12. Freud, *Civilization and Discontents*, 46–47.

N. T. Wright, expounded on the Freudian problem in his book *Simply Christian*. He states that there are many views like Freud's that tell us "spirituality is all the result of psychological forces . . . such as projecting a father-figure onto a cosmic screen. It's all imagination or wishful thinking or both."[13] The fact that people are hungry for spirituality does not prove anything about the actual existence of God according to thinkers like Nietzsche and Freud. But it should be noted here that, even if they differ in regard to why people have a divine hunger, both Freud and Nietzsche recognized that people are still inclined to have it regardless.

Dr. Robert Crapps thus summarizes Freud's theory: "The psychological origins of God reside in the continuous replay of the infantile dreams of collision between parent and child." If looked at in this light, "religion is a human attempt to cope with both instinctual demands and threats of pain and death written on a cosmic screen."[14]

To be sure, there is no question that both Freud and Nietzsche had creative ideas for the origin of humanity's desire for the divine. No one can deny the needs and desires humans have for security. It also makes sense that this innate sense of security would want to seek to extend beyond this world. The human instinct for survival naturally tends to project itself outward beyond death. Neither is there any denying the human tendency to deify the heroes of the world as Nietzsche suggests. In fact, one might argue that Nietzsche's superman is more qualified to serve as the illusive projection of the divine than Freud's father-figure.

But regardless of the differences, there are striking similarities between Nietzsche and Freud. In fact, most naturalist theories (including the many non-theistic evolutionary nuances) will share many of the basic ideas of these two authors. According to both, God is created by mankind to serve the human being's social and psychological needs. They both assume that humanity has a natural desire for transcendence. While Freud believed that religion was an "obsessional neurosis of humanity," he at least recognized that it was a "universal obsession" (i.e., a natural desire) nonetheless.[15] Thus, both authors stand in a long anthropological tradition that affirms humanity's desire to worship something greater. In

---

13. Wright, *Simply Christian*, 25.
14. Crapps, *Introduction*, 73.
15. Freud, *Future*, 43.

fact, these assumptions are well attested in literature throughout history.¹⁶ Charles Taliaferro has suggested that, "Arguably, a very general form of theism can be found in reported religious experiences in Judaism, Christianity, and Islam, and theistic traditions within Hinduism, Buddhism, African religions, Sikhism, aboriginal or primary religions, theistic Confucianism, and other religions."¹⁷ Kai-Man Kwan also affirms that,

> Since time immemorial, human beings in all of the major cultures or societies, there have been a great many reports of a great variety of RE's [Religious Experiences, J.P.]. The evidence for this claim can be garnered from the entire corpus of the religious literature in human history, which is evidently too voluminous to be summarized here. I trust that numerous basic texts on religious studies would substantiate this claim.¹⁸

But while it may be easily shown that humans are religious creatures, the question that remains to be answered, however, is whether or not theories such as the ones Freud and Nietzsche offer satisfy all the aspects concerning the existence of humanity's desire for transcendence. One may argue that while they provide certain *necessary* conditions that would be needed to account for the creation of God, they, nonetheless, are not *sufficient* conditions in light of humanity's more complex condition. Neither Freud's "father-figure" nor Nietzsche's "superman" (better translated "over-man") can satisfy humanity's real craving. Nietzsche and Freud's theories were inventive and creative, but they do not appear to have gone far enough. They bring humanity no closer to his ultimate desire. Rather than trying to satisfy humanity's desire for the divine, they seek to explain it away and attribute it to something illusionary. Theories like those of Freud and Nietzsche will only encourage men to live, as those of whom Lewis spoke, "like an ignorant child who wants to go on making mud pies in a slum because he cannot imagine what is meant by

---

16. See for instance Emile Durkheim's *Elementary Forms of Religious Life* in which he seeks to find the common denominator of religious belief throughout the ages, beginning with the most primitive society. While finding a sociological explanation of religion, Durkheim states that it is "incomprehensible" that religion could have survived for centuries if it were nothing but a "system of fictions" (71). He further states that "Our entire study rests on this postulate: that this unanimous feeling of believers across time cannot be purely illusory" (312).

17. Taliaferro, "Defense," 112.

18. Kwan, "Argument," 512.

the offer of a holiday at the sea."[19] Their theories were too shallow for what we find in the world and in the human heart. We should not think that the history of God can be explained by humanity's simple desire to fill their immediate need for safety. This shallow view of belief has been challenged by many psychologists and philosophers alike. Dr. Robert Crapps states, "With some justification they see Freud's definition of religion as quite narrow, restricted to beliefs and practices associated with the idea of a transcendent God operating in an authoritarian relationship to believers. He seems to have been unaware that religion comes in many forms and to have been content to treat threatening authoritarian religion as the entire picture."[20]

But whatever else we may say about Freud's views on God, he recognized the power that desire had to bear on the subject. While he had his theories on technology, God, and society, he never claimed to have the last word on it. He still did not believe that he had the final answer on life's discontentment and its unsatisfied hopes. He concluded *Civilization and Its Discontents* with a much more modest tone saying,

> One thing only do I know for certain and that is that man's judgments of value follow directly his wishes for happiness—that, accordingly, they are an attempt to support his illusions with arguments . . . Thus I have not the courage to rise up before my fellow-men as a prophet. And I bow to their reproach that I can offer them no consolation: for at bottom that is what they are all demanding—the wildest revolutionaries no less passionately than the most virtuous believers.[21]

And here comes his most pertinent point when he says, "Men have gained control over the forces of nature to such an extent that with their help they would have no difficulty in exterminating one another to the last man. They know this, and hence comes a large part of their current unrest, their unhappiness and their mood of anxiety."[22]

As true as he felt his views were, Freud knew there was more. There was always this ever present "unrest" and "anxiety" that no theory could remove. For Freud, desire for something more in order to remove this

---

19. Lewis, *Weight*, 26.
20. Crapps, *Introduction*, 72.
21. Freud, *Civilization and Discontents*, 154–55.
22. Ibid.

discontentment is never ending. Thus, his earlier stated view that there was nothing greater than a child's need for protection, and that this need could only be sought in parental relations, was far off the mark. If it were true, then nothing "more" would be needed indeed. But Freud was right to note humanity's discontentment. Nothing on earth fully satisfies the human condition.

So as creative as Nietzsche and Freud's views are, neither one adequately takes into account humanity's full spiritual and psychological condition. Neither theory properly acknowledges the multi-dimensional aspect of faith. Humanity's desire for the divine is far more complicated (not to mention sublime) than the explanation that makes the gods out to be heavenly hit men who are there to drive away the predators of life. Humanity longs for much more than security. In fact, the craving for the divine goes far deeper than can be compared to a superficial and immediate hunger that is satisfied by any one particular source in this world. People need more than a hero to fear, and they need more than a father-figure for protection. In fact, philosophers like Plato, St. Augustine, Blaise Pascal, St. Thomas and C. S. Lewis would argue that nothing at all in this world is encompassing enough to satisfy this intense craving. Freud's theory would have humanity create God merely out of a childish sense of wishful thinking. But, as will be spelled out in greater detail later, human cognitive faculties (such as intentionality, rationality, and memory) when properly functioning are generally *truth-aimed*. In other words, the human mind tends to want to take in only what is true and to weed out what is false. And it is out of these cognitive faculties that desire for transcendence springs.

Perhaps N. T. Wright is right to point out that this longing may very well "be the echo of a voice—a voice which is calling, not so loudly as to compel us to listen whether we choose to or not, but not so quietly as to be drowned out altogether by the noises going on in our heads and our world."[23] Thus the Argument from Desire allows us a rational choice between two conflicting worldviews. What follows is an exposition of how thinkers like C. S. Lewis used the argument as an attempt to move us closer to faith.

---

23. Wright, *Simply Christian*, 25.

CHAPTER 1

The Argument as Presented in Selected Works of C. S. Lewis

ALTHOUGH C. S. LEWIS never used the phrase "Argument from Desire," the argument itself fills the pages of many of his most cherished works. In fact, Lewis describes humanity's desire for God in many diverse and creative ways throughout his writings. Some of his most creative ways are found in his works of fiction, such as *Till We Have Faces*, *Perelandra*, *Pilgrim's Regress*, and his most famous works in the *Chronicles of Narnia*. But his most direct explanation of this desire comes from his works of non-fiction, such as *Mere Christianity*, *The Weight of Glory*, and *Surprised by Joy*. He also wrote what is considered by some to be one of the best short chapters on the subject of "Heaven" in *The Problem of Pain*, which relates to this intense longing for a heavenly home. Probably the best way to begin to describe Lewis's Argument from Desire (though, again, he never called it this) is to offer a brief description of what he says about it in some of his own works. For the sake of brevity and clarity, we will primarily focus our discussion toward his works of non-fiction, though we will later occasionally bring in illustrations from his works of fiction as well. In this chapter we will spend some time expositing the chapter entitled "Hope" in *Mere Christianity* and comparing it to the Afterword to the third edition of *The Pilgrim's Regress*. His other works like *Surprised by Joy*, *The Problem of Pain*, and *The Weight of Glory* (although mentioned here) will also be discussed in more detail in future chapters to further explain the argument. Later, we will also attempt to define a critical German word that Lewis associated with the kind of "Joy"[1] he sought to describe.

---

1. As will be discussed in detail in chapter 2, Lewis used the word "Joy" in a technical sense to describe man's intense longing for God. We must not confuse "joy" in the

The Apologetics of Joy

Mere Christianity and Lewis's Practical Presentation of the Argument

It may well be argued that in his chapter "Hope" in *Mere Christianity,* Lewis most succinctly (and practically) describes mankind's heavenly desire. He begins by saying that Christians have largely "ceased to think of the other world that they have become so ineffective in this. Aim at Heaven and you will get earth thrown in: aim at earth and you will get neither."[2] Lewis did not mean to assert that Christians no longer have the desire for heaven. Such a desire, according to Lewis, is so natural that one must *learn* to ignore it. However, while this desire is unavoidable, we often identify it with some other object. He makes the point that "our whole education tends to fix our minds on this world." Thus, "When the real want of Heaven is present with us, we do not recognize it. Most people, if they had really learned to look into their own hearts, would know that they do want, and want acutely, something that cannot be had in this world. There are all sorts of things in this world that offer to give it to you, but they never quite keep their promise."[3]

According to Lewis, since this desire is one that never truly gets satisfied on earth, there are three ways people often deal with it. One way is what Lewis calls the "Fool's Way." These people simply blame this unsatisfied desire on "things themselves." One goes through life,

> Thinking that if only he tried another woman, or went for a more expensive holiday, or whatever it is, then, this time, he really would catch the mysterious something we are after. Most of the bored, discontented, rich people in the world are of this type. They spend their whole lives trotting from woman to woman . . . from continent to continent, from hobby to hobby, always thinking that the latest is "the real thing" at last, and always disappointed.[4]

The Fool's Way is the most common way of dealing with this longing. It is the same avenue that the writer of Ecclesiastes took. As he sought to find the meaning of life, he tried to find it in all kinds of pleasures

---

normal sense of happiness or pleasure with the word "Joy" in the sense Lewis meant it. "Joy" in this Lewisian technical sense is capitalized throughout this book to distinguish it from "joy" in the usual sense.

2. Lewis, *Mere Christianity*, 134.
3. Ibid., 135.
4. Ibid., 135–36.

and goods. For example, he sought it in education (1:16–18), in wine and indulgence (2:1–8), and in occupation (2:17–24), just to name a few. But in his entire search he found nothing that filled the craving he had. Everything he sought to satisfy him seemed like "grasping for the wind," reaching outward but grabbing nothing. "Vanity of vanities, all is vanity," cries the writer (1:1–2).

But the problem for the writer of Ecclesiastes was the same problem for Lewis's Fool. They were both trying to find satisfaction for a desire that could not be fulfilled in this world. It was not until the end of Ecclesiastes that the writer finally found out what could fill his heart's desire. It was God he was after the whole time but did not know it (12:13–14). He had a longing for God even while he did not know that God was the true object of this longing.

Like Lewis, the writer of Ecclesiastes taught that God has put "eternity into our hearts" (3:11). But the only thing big enough to fill a hole the size of eternity is a proper object that is itself eternal. For both the writer in Ecclesiastes and Lewis, this object can only be God. Thus the Fool has placed his efforts in objects that can never satisfy him.

The second way some people try to explain this unsatisfied desire is what Lewis calls the "Way of the Disillusioned 'Sensible Man.'" There will be much more to say about this Sensible Man below. But Lewis would describe this person as one who has grown out of childish fairy tales. He "settles down and learns not to expect too much and represses the part of himself which used, as he would say, 'to cry for the moon.'" This man calls for "common sense" and believes only in tangible things. But again, we will have more to say about this person later.[5]

The third way of explaining this unsatisfied desire is the "Christian Way." Here is where Lewis suggests his own Argument from Desire most vividly.

> Creatures are not born with desires unless satisfaction for those desires exists. A baby feels hunger: well, there is such a thing as food. A duckling wants to swim: well, there is such a thing as water. Men feel sexual desire: well, there is such a thing as sex. If I find in myself a desire which no experience in this world can satisfy, the most probable explanation is that I was made for another world. If none of my earthly pleasures satisfy it, that does not prove that the

5. Ibid., 136.

universe is a fraud. Probably earthy pleasures were never meant to satisfy it, but only to arouse it, to suggest the real thing.[6]

Thus the Christian understanding of this unsatisfied desire is not that it is a mere child's wishful thinking. Nor is it something that simply lingers around luring humanity continuously into all forms of pleasures that never offer what he is really looking for. It would be a cruel thing indeed for nature to give us something useless. Nature would be the greatest tease of all to give us an unending desire for something that we never find to be real. It would be a strange view of natural selection to have evolved a desire for an object that has never existed. Natural selection only selects that which is useful to life. It gives us what we need in order to survive in our environment. But what use is having a desire that has nothing at all to do with our current environment? This is not to say that there are no plausible answers to this question. We will explore these options in part 4.

But this is exactly the point that Lewis is challenging. The usefulness of this longing comes from its pointing us to an environment not like the one we are currently in. Since, according to Lewis, all innate desires must have an existing object that correlates to that desire, there must be something that exists to satisfy our currently unsatisfied desire. To better understand what Lewis is doing, we might compare him to an earlier work written by Rudolf Otto that influenced Lewis's thinking on this subject.

Otto's Haunted World and its Influence on Lewis's Argument

Otto was a German theologian and philosopher of comparative religions. In *The Idea of the Holy*, Otto examined the experience of the divine much like what Lewis sought to accomplish. Though a case may be made that no one defended the Argument from Desire as stridently as Lewis, elements of his views are foreshadowed in works such as Otto's.

While some have "interpreted aesthetics in term of sensuous pleasures, and religion as a function of the gregarious instinct and social standards," Otto seeks to find the answers to these questions in what he calls the "numinous." While thinkers such as Friedrich Schleiermacher are right to find that much by way of religious conviction comes from a "feeling of dependence," Otto believes it is more than this. The difference between having a sense of the divine and other kinds of feelings is a

6. Ibid., 137.

qualitative difference and not just a difference of degrees. While our sense of the divine does come from a "feeling of dependence," it is not "*merely* a feeling of dependence." It comes from what Otto calls, "creature-consciousness" or "creature-feeling."[7]

For Otto, this creature-consciousness is the "emotion of a creature, submerged and overwhelmed by its own nothingness in contrast to that which is supreme above all creatures." This creature-feeling is "itself a first subjective concomitant and effect of another feeling-element, which casts it like a shadow, but which in itself indubitably has immediate and primary reference to an object outside the self."[8] This sense is what Otto calls the "numinous." Rather than simply a subjective sense of dependence, the "numinous" is felt as "objective and outside" the self. It is a sense in which we are being watched (or haunted). Peter Kreeft tries to capture the word by describing it as follows:

> The sense that the world we see is haunted by something we do not see, an unseen presence. It often inspires awe and fear because it is not humanly predictable and controllable, not definable and tamable. It seems to come from another dimension, another *kind* of reality, than the world it haunts. It is the primitive wonder that is the source of fairy tales and myths and also of the instinct of worship.[9]

While there are many hints at this "haunting" of our world, Kreeft poetically suggests that even the "whole world seems to be a face" that haunts us every day. Sometimes we feel this sense more so than other times and, like anything else, people can learn to ignore this sense of presence in life even to the point of rejecting it was ever there altogether. Lewis explains this "haunting" in his chapter on heaven, saying, "All your life an unattainable ecstasy has hovered just beyond the grasp of your consciousness." This hovering "ecstasy" will be something that one has either "attained" in the afterlife or, though it was always within reach, "lost forever."[10]

One word of explanation needs to be made before moving any further. While there are many similarities between Otto and Lewis, and while

---

7. Otto, *Idea*, 9–10.
8. Ibid.
9. Kreeft, *Heaven*, 97–98.
10. Lewis, *Problem*, 32

The Apologetics of Joy

it is helpful to think of the "numinous" as it can relate to Lewis's "Joy," there is one difference that needs to be noted. This difference is summarized in what Robert Holyer says in his article titled "The Argument from Desire." "Joy lacks precisely what Otto regarded essential to the holy, and that is a sense of the divine presence. As Lewis described it, Joy is not an awareness of God's presence; it is simply unfulfilled desire."[11] Yet even with this difference, Joy is related to this sense of presence in such a way that we can be prompted along toward transcendence by means of it. Like the numinous, Joy cannot be located in anything earthly. While the numinous is the feeling of divine presence, Joy is the craving and search for it. Yet, in both cases, one may feel the desire or the haunting without identifying the object of it.

Before we rush to judge Lewis and Otto's views as mere mystical phenomenon, it is important to keep clear in mind the connection of this divine sense to ordinary life. Peter Berger is helpful here when he speaks in a similar vein as Lewis and Otto concerning what he calls the "signals of transcendence." Because the Argument from Desire appeals to humanity's internal needs and longings, it is tempting to equate it with mere internal, *a priori*, feelings and illusions that spring from childhood subconscious insecurities. This, again, is what Freud would have us think of religion: mere childish wishful thinking springing from uncontrollable fears. But while justification of the Argument from Desire cannot be empirically proven in the same manner that hyper-empirical scientific methods would look for, the argument does nonetheless suggest itself within the empirical world. The argument is best seen as an inductive argument that rests, not solely on "mysterious revelation, but rather on what we experience in our common, ordinary lives."[12]

So according to Berger, it is the ordinary things of life combined with a real divine presence that connect us to this numinous feeling. These "signals of transcendence" are not themselves the things desired, however. They are hints that something beyond this world is there. In his own autobiographical sketch of his journey toward Joy, Lewis explains that, "authentic Joy . . . is distinct not only from pleasure in general but even from aesthetic pleasure. It must have the stab, the pang, the inconsolable longing."[13] In this way, the Joy Lewis spoke of is not always expressed as

11. Holyer, "Argument," 26.
12. Berger, *Rumor*, 60.
13. Lewis, *Surprised*, 72.

a feeling of pleasure. "It might almost equally well be called a particular kind of unhappiness or grief."[14] But strangely it is a kind of grief that we want. It is a pain like we feel when we are separated from someone we have loved more than anything or anyone else. For Lewis, we "ache" in desire because we have a sense that there exists a love greater than anything in this world. It is a kind of unhappiness felt like one feels because of homesickness. The difference is that this feeling of homesickness is for a home we have never been to or seen before.

Thus, in *Mere Christianity* Lewis presents the Argument from Desire from a practical and inductive approach. It is in the Afterword to the third edition of *The Pilgrim's Regress* that Lewis lays out what he means by it in a more analytical and definitive way.

Pilgrim's Regress and Lewis's Direct Approach to the Argument

In the Afterword, Lewis says that the desire he is speaking of is different from other desires in at least two ways. First, "though the sense of want is acute and even painful, yet the mere wanting is felt to be somehow a delight."[15] The very feeling of transcendent desire is itself a form of Joy. The longing for the satisfaction is itself a kind of satisfaction. Maybe the best way we can capture what Lewis is saying is to compare it to the word "hope." Often people will be able to endure present hardships with greater strength when they have in themselves a sense that there is something more to be valued and anticipated beyond the current situation. Hope itself is a cherished feeling even beyond the expected events hoped for. The difference still being, however, that hope has this value insofar as it points to the known expected future event. Whereas, "other desires are felt as pleasures only if satisfaction is expected in the near future,"[16] Joy, as Lewis understood it, was pleasurable even when the satisfaction was not foreseeable. This makes Joy a kind of desire that is itself euphoric. It is as if, as Lewis put it, "this hunger is better than any other fullness."[17] It is a feeling of "want" that keeps us inspired and moving toward something

14. Ibid., 18.
15. Lewis, *Regress*, 202.
16. Ibid.
17. Ibid.

even when we do not know what that something is. For Lewis, this desire is a divine desire for something that transcends anything that is in front of us or around us. We long for it, in part, because of the mystery and excitement it brings to life. We desire it because we feel that there is more to life than what meets the eye. It gives us a sense that, whatever it is, it is bigger than the here and now. Thus, we cherish the desire itself, even without its satisfaction. This is why Lewis called this desire "Joy." It offers Joy even without any final satisfaction that normally accompanies typical joy.

The second way that this heavenly desire (i.e., "Joy") is different than all other desires is that, in the case of other desires, a person knows the object that he/she desires. We alluded to it above, but we need to specify this point here. Lewis believed that the object of this superior desire is, *when it stands by itself*, unidentifiable. Lewis expresses it this way,

> There is a peculiar mystery about the object of this Desire. Inexperienced people (and inattention leaves some inexperienced all their lives) suppose, when they feel it, that they know what they are desiring. Thus if it comes to a child while he is looking at a far off hillside he at once thinks "if only I were there"; if it comes when he is remembering some event in the past, he thinks "if only I could go back to those days." If it comes (a little later) while he is reading a "romantic" tale or poem of "perilous seas and faerie lands forlorn," he thinks he is wishing that such places really existed and that he could reach them. If it comes (later still) in a context with erotic suggestions he believes he is desiring the perfect beloved. If he falls upon literature (like Maeterlinck or the early Yeats) which treats of spirits and the like with some show of serious belief, he may think that he is hankering for real magic and occultism. When it darts out upon him from his studies in history or science, he may confuse it with the intellectual craving for knowledge. But every one of these impressions is wrong . . . Every one of these supposed objects for the Desire is inadequate to it.[18]

With these points in mind, it needs to be kept clear that when one speaks of the Argument from Desire as pointing to the existence of God, one is not saying that those who experience this desire know that God is what they desire. What is being asserted here, as will be laid out more carefully later, is that since there is nothing on earth (i.e., no identifiable object) that satisfies this desire (and that since all natural desires have objects that satisfy them) then there must be some transcendent object

18. Ibid., 203.

like God that exists. Thus, the success of the argument does not depend upon anyone being able to directly identify the object of this mysterious, albeit natural desire. It only depends upon the premises that will be more clearly laid out below. Before moving on to that objective there is one more essential ingredient that will help clarify the kind of Joy that Lewis describes.

CHAPTER 2

Defining Joy as *Sehnsucht*

IT IS OBVIOUS FROM the proceeding chapter that when Lewis spoke of Joy he did not at all mean what we typically mean when we say the word. It is neither an emotion nor a mere sentimental feeling. It is not some feeling we get when we look at a painting or when we hear an uplifting song. It is rather that intense sense we have when, in looking at a painting or hearing a song, we know and long for something more; something greater than what we are seeing or hearing. Aesthetic feeling is the feeling we get when we are content or satisfied with the beauty of people or things. When we usually use the word "joy" we usually are thinking of something that is pleasant or satisfying and we almost always know what is bringing us this feeling. The key here is that joy, in the usual sense, refers to something (usually identifiable) that *removes* any discontentment. However, Lewis's word "Joy" is more like appreciation for all that is beautiful and inspiring on earth *even while* in a state of uneasy discontentment with it. To best communicate what he was trying to say when using the word "Joy," Lewis uses the German word *Sehnsucht* to describe it.[1] For Lewis, *Sehnsucht* is "an unsatisfied desire which is itself more desirable than any other satisfaction. I call it Joy, which is here a technical term and must be sharply distinguished both from Happiness and from Pleasure. Joy (in my sense) has indeed one characteristic, and one only, in common with them; the fact that anyone who has experienced it will want it again."[2]

1. Lewis, *Surprised*, 7.
2. Ibid., 17–18.

Distinguishing Between "joy" and "Joy"

To illustrate the distinction between ordinary joy and Lewis's Joy, we can compare it to the experience of marriage. Even when someone is in the healthiest marriage he/she still can never get *enough* of his/her spouse's love. In a healthy marriage there never comes a day when a wife says, "My husband has given me *enough* love, therefore I do not need any more of it." In this way, Lewis's Joy is similar to the desire of getting or being married. There is always the feeling of wanting more. The key difference between the desire to get married and Joy, however, is that when a person truly longs to get married they do not get any joy from the desire *itself*. They only seek pleasure in its *fulfillment*. I write this after having left the hospital because a church member's wife just passed away. As I stood and watched her exhale her last breath and saw her heart rate go from forty to thirty-five, to twenty, to zero, there was nothing but sadness in the room. The tears from the husband's eyes told me that he would never get *enough* of his wife's love. He wanted more. He would always want more. This is the world we live in. A world that never offers us enough of what we are really after. It is not the joy of *wanting* to get married we want, it is marriage *itself*. The problem is that, like everything else that brings us pleasure in life, marriage does not last forever. It brings us joy, but it does not bring us Joy. Sure, joyful experiences in life can point us in the direction of Joy (as we shall see), but it cannot give us what we eternally long for. They always come up short. The same is true for music, food, art, children, and everything else good in our world.

This description brings in another element to Lewis's definition that was only mentioned above in passing. Ironically, for Lewis, since this longing is never fully satisfied on earth, Joy becomes both the continual act of desiring as well as the thing being desired itself. When contemplating whether it was aesthetic experience he was after, Lewis realized that it was nothing even close to it. Personifying the Joy he had sought, he states that, "Inexorably Joy proclaimed, 'You want—I myself am your want of—something other, outside, not you nor any state of you.' I did not yet ask, Who is the desired? only What is it?" What Lewis found, which he had been so longing for, had nothing at all to do with any object in this world. It was no social or biological need that could satisfy him. In fact, nothing "clothed in our senses" would ever qualify to do the job.[3]

3. Ibid., 221.

The Apologetics of Joy

One of the most illustrative of Lewis's descriptions of this *Sehnsucht* (i.e., Joy) comes from an unexplained reference in *Surprised by Joy*. It is a reference to a relatively unknown literary work that most readers of Lewis would not have read.[4]

To help with this briefly referenced work, Alan Jacobs expounds on it in his book *The Narnian*. The literary piece is an unfinished novel by the German Romantic writer Friedrich von Hardenberg, entitled *Heinrich Von Ofterdingen*. According to Jacobs, the protagonist of the novel,

> Becomes obsessed by a vision of a blue flower, which he first encounters in a stranger's tales and then in dreams:
> "There is no greed in my heart; but I yearn to get a glimpse of the blue flower [*aber die blaue Blume sehn' ich mich zu erblicken*]. It is perpetually in my mind, and I can write or think of nothing else . . .
> Often I feel so rapturously happy; and only when I do not have the flower clearly before my mind's eye does a deep inner turmoil seize me. This cannot and will not be understood by anyone. I would think I were mad if I did not see and think so clearly. Indeed since then everything is much clearer to me."
> He "yearns" or "longs" (*sehn*) for the flower—and yet nothing that he can grasp seems so desirable as that longing itself. This is the paradox of *Sehnsucht*: that though it could in one sense be described as a negative experience, in that it focuses on something one cannot possess and cannot reach, it is nevertheless intensely seductive. One cannot say exactly pleasurable—there is a kind of ache in the sense of unattainability that always accompanies the longing.[5]

It is for this reason that Lewis speaks of "an unsatisfied desire which is itself more desirable than any other satisfaction."[6] It is called Joy, according to Jacobs, because "the word *longing* fails to convey the desirability of the feeling itself."[7] While people usually do not want to be in a state of unsatisfied longing, they do wish to experience the currently unsatisfied longing of Joy. It is a kind of divine drug that keeps us coming back for more.

---

4. Ibid., 7.
5. Jacobs, *Narnian*, 41.
6. Lewis, *Surprised*, 17.
7. Jacobs, *Narnian*, 41.

Defining Joy as Sehnsucht

Apparently this blue "flower motif" is a characteristic feature of Romantic literature. According to Corbon Scott Carnell, this motif is a "compulsive quest or 'pursuit of the unattainable' which causes a certain amount of pleasure itself but ultimately a sense of sadness due to the unattainable nature of what is desired."[8] Carnell explained that "whenever we find the romantic attitude in its most intense form, we may very well find *Sehnsucht*."[9] Thus, the literary evidence points us toward defining *Sehnsucht* broadly as an intense and pleasurable longing for what we do not yet have.

Elaborating on the Definition of Sehnsucht a Bit More

These literary elements of *Sehnsucht* are consistent with how other sources (such as those looking at it from a purely psychological perspective) define the word. Yet the difficulty of defining *Sehnsucht* in English is expressed by Mayser, Scheibe, and Riediger, saying that "Because the word *Sehnsucht* has no precise English translation, the authors opted for the term 'life longings' to express its holistic character."[10] However, these authors recognize that translating *Sehnsucht* as "life longings" does not do the word full justice. As will be seen below, they saw that the word carried many possible aspects within its meaning.

Additionally consistent with what Lewis taught, these authors also affirm the universality and natural quality of the experience of *Sehnsucht* saying, "Despite the difficulty of translating *Sehnsucht* into English, the basic thoughts and feelings associated with this phenomenon are likely relevant for many people's recurring thoughts and feelings, not only in Germany."[11] But despite the difficulty of translation, the authors pose a number of qualities that are believed to be involved in this rich German word. For our purposes we discuss three of their most relevant points for our study:

First, life longings (i.e., *Sehnsucht*) are "proposed to involve a sense of incompleteness of one's life. This realization of imperfection in one's actual life, which arises in the context of losses, non-chosen alternatives,

---

8. Connolly, *Inklings*, 52.
9. Ibid.
10. Mayser et al., "(Un)Reachable?" 126.
11. Ibid.

or blocked life paths, is regarded as the origin of life's longings."[12] While Lewis would not necessarily agree with their assertions concerning the "origins" of the "longings," there would be full agreement with the description itself. The sense of Joy or *Sehnsucht* is experienced because, although life is not perfect, there is a hope in the human spirit that it somehow can (or *should*) be.

Second, "life longings are assumed to comprise personal utopias, or mental images of one's ideal life."[13] Again, Lewis thought that this element of our longing arises from the fact that man's "ideal life" has been lost in the Fall (Gen 3). Of course, many evolutionary psychologists believe that this utopian world is merely a creation of man's imagination. While Lewis would agree that utopia is within the grasp of human imagination (see chapter 11 of this book), he would argue that it is only there because such a utopian world exists in the first place. Our self-imposed loss of access to the Garden of Eden has simply put us in a position to fail to fully experience and access that Ideal World.

Third, "life longings are conceptualized as having an ambivalent emotional quality. The incompleteness and unattainability on the one hand, and the fantasy of one's ideal life on the other, are assumed to lead to a 'bittersweet' experience, a blend of positive and negative emotions."[14] Lewis's position on this has been explained in detail above. But it is sufficient to say at this point that Lewis believed this negative and positive feeling of ambivalence is due to not having access to the awe-inspiring world (i.e., ideal life) that we yet crave and look for.

To put all of the above elements together into one definition we might say that *Sehnsucht* is "the aching, and yet pleasurable, intense longing for a life that we cannot yet have but naturally and universally crave. It is the feeling of having lost something that we once had—giving us a sense of homesickness and discontentment with the less-than-ideal world we currently find ourselves in."

Thus, for Lewis, because of its universality, *Sehnsucht* is a kind of pleading of the world. It is reminiscent of Paul's expression in Romans that, because of sin, "the whole creation groans and labors with birth pangs together . . ." anticipating its coming salvation (Rom 8:22). This

12. Ibid., 127.
13. Ibid.
14. Ibid.

longing is a natural one due to our current loss and desire for divine fellowship and ideal home where no death or sorrow exists. Alluding to Lewis's work *Out of the Silent Planet*, Jacobs states that "*Sehnsucht* is the mood of our world: the *Silent Planet* (i.e., *earth*, J.P.) longs for connection, for restoration of the music of the other spheres from which we have cut ourselves off."[15]

Nevertheless, because the object of *Sehnsucht* is, on one hand, *unknown* without special revelation (such as the Bible) and, on the other hand, something *naturally experienced*, we must explain the tension between these two elements. In other words, how can the acceptance of the Argument from Desire be *rationally* justified (especially for the atheist and agnostic) in light of the apparent absurdity of desiring to have an ideal life that we have never *seen* or *experienced* before? How can we bring together the *concrete feeling* we have of longing for this ideal life and having never *experienced* firsthand the mystery of this very life we so desire? To word the question more simply: how do we know it isn't all just in our heads?

---

15. Jacobs, "Chronicles," 278.

Chapter 3

Plantinga and Lewis: Balancing the Mystical and the Natural in *Sehnsucht*

A BRIEF COMPARISON OF the apologist Alvin Plantinga to C. S. Lewis might help to clarify what Lewis means when he speaks of having a natural desire for an object we cannot yet identify. It will be helpful to first compare the similarities to Lewis's "innate desire" with what Plantinga terms "properly basic beliefs."[1]

While Plantinga teaches that faith in God is properly basic, this does not mean that it is completely groundless. Because belief in God is properly basic it needs no further formal justifying evidence. Even so, this belief is not arbitrary but finds warrant in some underlying cause that makes

---

1. A "properly basic belief" is one where the person believes something that does not need any added evidence to support it. For example, the fact that we believe that other minds exist besides our own is a properly basic belief. I cannot prove to myself that other people are conscious besides me. I can only experience my own consciousness. Nevertheless, the vast majority of humans think that it is perfectly rational to believe that other people are conscious besides themselves. We do not need to see *proof* of this. Of course, there are actually some who do believe that they are the only conscious beings alive. They believe that every other person in their life is simply a part of their own dream-like state. This is called *solipsism*. But we generally consider these people to be unwarranted (if not a little crazy) in their belief even if we cannot prove them wrong with formal evidence. We can only share our testimony to them that we are conscious beings too. But if a solipsist really believes that he/she is the only conscious being, this will *prove* nothing to him/her. For all he/she knows, you are a part of their dream-like state and cannot be trusted. Another classic example of a properly basic belief is the fact that we all believe that our past has existed. While you cannot *prove* that you are not in an experimental room right now where scientists are feeding false memories and experiences into your brain, you still take it on face value that this is not happening to you. It is a properly basic belief that your past existed. Again, no one needs to *prove* this to you. Properly basic beliefs are also called "first principles" because there is nothing that we need to believe that would serve as prior justifying factors for them.

it reasonable to hold the belief. According to Plantinga, the ground for properly basic beliefs is its justifying circumstances. When our cognitive faculties (e.g., memory, intentionality, and rationality, etc.) are functioning properly within the right kind of environment that is suited for these functions, then the tendency is to hold the correct belief. This is not to say that it is impossible to deny what is properly basic. But it is the denial of these properly basic beliefs that is irrational and not the affirmation of such. As such, "What confers warrant is the proper function of faculties aimed at the production of true beliefs; when such beliefs are overridden by beliefs that are the result of the proper function of modules not aimed at truth (wishful thinking, for example) the resulting beliefs do not have warrant."[2]

Thus, according to Plantinga, God has made us in such a way that certain experiences in life trigger a natural tendency or disposition to believe in God. Plantinga sees this tendency as having been impaired due to the effects of sin. Humanity's noetic structure has been affected by the Fall of Genesis 3 in such a way that either the environment or humanity's cognitive functions have been altered.[3] Nevertheless, God has placed in humanity's created nature a *sensus divinitatis* (i.e., having a natural sense of the existence of something divine).[4] In the spirit of Aquinas and Calvin, Plantinga defines this phrase as referring to "a disposition or set of dispositions to form theistic beliefs in various circumstances, in response to the sorts of conditions or stimuli that trigger the working of this sense of divinity."[5]

We will see that this idea suggests that Lewis and Plantinga have much in common. For Plantinga, faith does not come through formal deductive reasoning alone (if at all). Faith is not a matter of having absolute certainty, as in the manner of extreme foundational internalism, such

2. Plantinga, *Warrant and Function*, 42.
3. Plantinga, *Belief*, 213–16.
4. One way of thinking of this *sensus divinitatis* is to compare it to an internal navigating system in the brain. As long as the system is working right we should rely on where it is taking us, even if we do not know all the reasons why it may be taking us there. The *sensus divinitatis* is a type of internal navigating system that leads humans naturally to faith. This does not remove the need for special revelation (such as the Bible). It only gives us a head start in our search for God. Although general revelation (like the beautiful world we live in) can tell us a lot about the Creator (cf. Ps 19:1 and Rom 1:20), only special revelation can tell us in detail which God we are supposed to be looking for.
5. Ibid., 173.

as what Descartes sought to achieve.[6] Plantinga is not opposed to formal arguments; he simply sees them as unnecessary to come to saving faith. Additionally, Plantinga believes that there are good rational arguments for God. Yet these arguments simply confirm what the individual may already be predisposed toward. Thus, for Plantinga, the natural inclination for humanity is to believe in God (or at least something we might call "divine").

Consequently, this is one of the failures of Freud's psychoanalytical explanation for belief described above in the introduction to part 1. Again, Freud held that humanity's belief in God was a form of mere wishful thinking. While some beliefs are held for this reason for certain people, it cannot be true of mankind universally, especially not for properly basic beliefs. Thus, according to Plantinga's view, Freud's wishful thinking cannot account for humanity's natural tendency to believe. Plantinga suggests that wishful thinking is not what humanity's cognitive functions (such as memory, intentionality, and rationality) are naturally geared toward. These human cognitive faculties are, in fact, "truth-aimed" generally. Even when we have believed in false objects such as Santa Claus, it is both the environment (i.e., the parents telling them so) that is at fault combined with the child's developing (and, consequently, limited) cognitive faculties. But while wishful thinking can override mankind's natural cognitive functions, it cannot *explain* them. This is a crucial difference between Freud and Plantinga. Nevertheless, insofar as the environment is conducive to humanity's truth-aimed faculties, we have a natural tendency toward true beliefs as long as our faculties are working properly (e.g., there is no mental illness) and we are not motivated by other emotional factors that get in the way. So while this tendency is not infallible, it offers us a reliable ground for rationality.

Thus, for Plantinga, while formal arguments may be helpful toward faith, they are not necessary. Karl Rahner makes a similar case when he argues that,

> A theoretical proof for the existence of God, then, is only intended to mediate a reflexive awareness of the fact that man always and inevitably has to do with God in his intellectual and spiritual

---

6. Descartes believed that one could only be certain that something was true or real (and, thus, justified to believe it) *only* if one had the kind of formal evidence that made it logically impossible to deny it. Both Lewis and Plantinga denied such a claim for the reasons explained in this chapter.

Plantinga and Lewis: Balancing the Mystical and the Natural in Sehnsucht

> existence, whether he reflects upon it or not, and whether he freely accepts it or not. The peculiar situation of giving the grounds subsequently for something which actually does the grounding and is already present, namely, the holy mystery, is what constitutes the specific character, the self-evident nature, and the difficulty of giving a reflexive proof for God's existence. That which does the grounding is itself grounded, as it were, and what is present in silence and without a name is itself given a name.[7]

In other words, like Plantinga, Rahner believes that formal arguments for God's existence only serve to "mediate" what can already be known through "reflexive awareness" of the "holy mystery." While we may come to know God *a posteriori* (i.e., through life's experiences), we interpret our experiences in light of what comes natural to our being. As Rahner has made the point already before this, that while it does not destroy the "*a posteriori* character of the knowledge of God" we are still "oriented towards God" by our "transcendent" nature.[8]

Lewis and Plantinga:
Making the Epistemological Connection

While it might be argued by some that Lewis placed a greater emphasis on formal argumentation, his Argument from Desire can be shown to assume something like what both Plantinga and Rahner are saying. On the one hand, according to Lewis, the object of the longing we have is not something that is found anywhere in our experiences in the world (i.e., "It is a desire for something that has never actually appeared in our experience").[9] In this way the desire must be one that is natural to our being *a priori* (i.e., to our natural cognitive faculties). Lewis suggests this also in *The Problem of Pain* when, in commenting on Otto's "numinous," he says that "this reaction is indeed 'natural' in the sense of being in accord with human nature."[10] In *The Weight of Glory* he says, "Now, if we are made for heaven, the desire for our proper place *will already be in us* . . ."[11] So, like Plantinga, Lewis held that human

---

7. Rahner, *Foundations*, 69.
8. Ibid., 53.
9. Lewis, *Weight*, 30.
10. Lewis, *Problem*, 17.
11. Lewis, *Weight*, 29. Italics mine.

31

cognitive faculties (such as laws of rational thought, intentionality, and inference) are naturally truth-aimed. In his essay "Man or Rabbit" Lewis more clearly expresses this: "One of the things that distinguishes man from the animals is that he wants to know things, wants to find out what reality is really like, simply for the sake of knowing. When that desire is completely quenched in anyone, I think he has become something less than human."[12]

On the other hand, like Plantinga, Lewis also believed that our environment offers a place where our natural tendencies are reinforced and allowed to be pointed further toward this mysterious object of desire. Thus, "We cannot hide it because our experience is constantly suggesting it."[13] In this sense our desire for God is *a posteriori* (i.e., motivated and informed by life's experiences).

Consequently, like Plantinga suggests, both our truth-aimed cognitive faculties as well as our environment must be properly functioning in order for a belief to be warranted. With these functions in place, *Sehnsucht* is able to impress itself upon us through the *sensus divinitatis*. In other words, the sense of wonder we have when we look at the "images of our desire," such as a mountain or a flower, can strike in us this longing for still something more, something divine. These "things," says Lewis, are only a "scent of a flower we have not found, the echo of a tune we have not heard, news from a country we have never yet visited."[14] In a sense, it is both natural and unnatural. It is natural because it comes to us through our inner and outer faculties; it is unnatural because it is a desire for something we have not *actually* experienced in nature. Nature testifies to *Sehnsucht* but does not finally satisfy it.

The connection between Plantinga's *sensus divinitatis* and Lewis's *Sehnsucht* become more evident when Plantinga explains that,

> The operation of the *sensus divinitatis* will always involve the presence of experience of some kind or other, even if sensuous imagery isn't always present. Sometimes there is sensuous imagery; sometimes there is something like feeling the presence of God, where there seems to be no sensuous imagery present, but perhaps something (necessarily hard to explain) *like* it; often there is also the sort of experience that goes with being frightened, feeling

12. Lewis, *God*, 108.
13. Lewis, *Problem*, 30.
14. Lewis, *Weight*, 31.

Plantinga and Lewis: Balancing the Mystical and the Natural in Sehnsucht

grateful, delighted foolish, angry, pleased, and the like. A common component is a sort of awe, a sense of the numinous; a sense of being in the presence of a being of overwhelming majesty and greatness.[15]

According to Plantinga, this is at least one way of experiencing the *sensus divinitatis* and it is very much like what Lewis and Otto are saying. But the key here is that while the *sensus divinitatis* (*Sehnsucht* for Lewis) is mysterious, it is also natural and universal to the human condition.

Alvin Plantinga, Uncle Andrew, and the Talking Beasts

There is a scene in *The Magician's Nephew*, from Lewis's Chronicles of Narnia series, that vividly illustrates the point of what we are discussing in this chapter. In the scene, four main characters, Digory, Polly, Uncle Andrew, and Frank the Cabby, are witnessing Aslan, the Lion (the character that represents Christ in the story), creating the world of Narnia. Everyone except Uncle Andrew is amazed by the miracles. But as soon as the beasts that Aslan creates begin to speak, Uncle Andrew refuses to believe it. In fact, after hearing Aslan singing, Uncle Andrew rationalizes it away. "'Of course, it can't really have been singing.' He thought, 'I must have imagined it. I've been letting my nerves get out of order. Who ever heard of a lion singing?'"[16] Thinking in light of Plantinga's views described above, the trouble with Uncle Andrew was that he refused to believe his own properly working mental faculties. He saw the lion creating Narnia. He had heard the animals speaking. And his *initial* thinking immediately disposed him to accept the reality of the situation. But, because of his pre-existing skepticism and his cynical mindset, he refused to believe what should have been otherwise natural for him to believe. Part of his problem was that he was the kind of man who had "never liked animals at the best of times, being usually afraid of them; and of course years of doing cruel experiments on animals had made him hate and fear them far more."[17]

An important point of this story is that there is more to what a person believes than mere intellectual curiosity and how much formal

15. Plantinga, *Belief*, 183.
16. Lewis, *Magician's Nephew*, 75.
17. Ibid., 76.

The Apologetics of Joy

evidence one has in favor of a claim. There is a moral element to *why* a person believes or disbelieves. Lewis observes, "For what you see and hear depends a good deal on where you are standing; it also depends on what sort of person you are . . . Now the trouble about trying to make yourself stupider than you really are is that you very often succeed. Uncle Andrew did. He soon did hear nothing but the roaring in Aslan's song. Soon he couldn't have heard anything else even if he wanted to."[18]

But the critical point that is here being illustrated with Uncle Andrew cuts to the very heart of what Alvin Plantinga was saying about what makes a person warranted in their beliefs. Uncle Andrew's mental faculties were working properly and were naturally truth-aimed. Additionally, there was nothing wrong in Uncle Andrew's environmental circumstances that should have led him to think he was dreaming or hallucinating. Thus, Uncle Andrew's cynicism was unjustified. However, his belief and acceptance of the situation would have been sufficiently warranted.

Many of these natural elements of Joy will be addressed in greater detail in part 4. For now, it is only mentioned and illustrated in this chapter to draw the reader's attention to this element of Lewis's concept of *Sehnsucht*. In part 4 we will further develop these ideas and how they apply to the evolutionary objection against the Argument from Desire. Suffice it to be said here that our human cognitive faculties appear to be *designed* to serve as warrant-enabling and truth-aimed mechanisms that point humanity toward the longing for God that Lewis envisioned. In other words, Uncle Andrew should have believed simply because it was natural and rational for him to do so.

18. Ibid., 75–76.

Chapter 4

A Word on the Different Forms that the Argument Can Take

WHILE SOME READERS WILL see this chapter as merely academic in nature, it does serve an important purpose for our study. To more clearly identify all the pieces of the argument, we will benefit from looking at the different ways that the argument can be presented formally. Doing this also helps us to see not only the validity of the argument, but it will also help us later on to evaluate how strong the argument is.

Deductive or Inductive? Is That Really the Question?

Some readers of Lewis have observed two distinct forms that the Argument from Desire can take: inductive or deductive.[1] In *Mere Christianity* and *Weight of Glory* Lewis can be read to offer a slightly softer (or inductive) approach to the argument. In *Mere Christianity* he says,

> Creatures are not born with desires unless satisfaction for those desires exists. A baby feels hunger: well, there is such a thing as food. A duckling wants to swim: well, there is such a thing as water. Men feel sexual desire: well, there is such a thing as sex. If I find in myself a desire which no experience in this world can satisfy, the most probable explanation is that I was made for another world. If none of my earthy pleasures satisfy it, that does not prove that the

---

1. A deductive argument occurs if the supporting premises (or propositions) of the argument are true and thus prove the conclusion *must* also be true. An inductive argument happens when the supporting premises of an argument confer a certain degree of *probability* to the conclusion.

> universe is a fraud. Probably earthy pleasures were never meant to satisfy it, but only to arouse it, to suggest the real thing.[2]

Notice he says that since he has a desire for something not found in this world then the "most probable explanation" is that I was made for another world. In this sense Lewis believes that his case is a strong case in which the conclusion (while not necessary) is "most probable." He does something similar in *The Weight of Glory* when he says,

> We remain conscious of a desire which no natural happiness will satisfy. But is there any reason to suppose that reality offers any satisfaction of it? . . . A man's physical hunger does not prove that any man will get any bread; he may die of starvation on a raft in the Atlantic. But surely a man's hunger does prove that he comes of a race which repairs its body by eating and inhabits a world where eatable substances exist. In the same way, though I do not believe . . . that my desire for Paradise proves that I shall enjoy it, I think it a pretty good indication that such a thing exists and that some men will.[3]

Notice again when he reaches his conclusion he states that it is a "pretty good indication" that such a thing as Paradise exists. As Kreeft explains, "Lewis does not claim certainty for the conclusion here, just probability. For the conclusion here is only a hypothesis that explains the data better than any other, but this fact does not prove with certainly that this hypothesis is true."[4]

Though, again, while not wanting to make too much of it, in the Afterword of the *Pilgrim's Regress* Lewis words his case more strongly (i.e., deductively) saying,

> It appeared to me therefore that if a man diligently followed this desire, pursuing the false objects until their falsity appeared and then resolutely abandoning them, he must come out at last into the clear knowledge that the human soul was made to enjoy some object that is never fully given—nay, cannot even be imagined as given—in our present mode of subjective and spatio-temporal experience. This Desire was, in the soul, as the Siege Perilous in Arthur's caste—the chair in which only one could sit. And if

---

2. Lewis, *Mere Christianity*, 137.
3. Lewis, *Weight*, 32–33.
4. Kreeft, *Heaven*, 208.

A Word on the Different Forms that the Argument Can Take

nature makes nothing in vain, the One who can sit in this chair must exist.[5]

Notice the stronger statements made such as "he *must* come out at last to a clear knowledge" and "the One who can sit in the chair *must* exist." Again, one should not make too much of all this. The differences may simply reflect Lewis's recognition that the argument, while very strong in his mind, cannot give us absolute certainty. But again, since some have found in these quotes two clear ways of arguing for his case, the point is mentioned here. It may be helpful to spell out a few of the ways the argument can be formulated.

A deductive form of the argument offered by John Beversluis in his critical book *C. S. Lewis and the Search for Rational Religion* is as follows:

1. Nature makes nothing in vain; that is, every natural desire has an object that can satisfy it.
2. Joy is a natural desire, but not for any natural object because no object in the natural world can satisfy it.
3. Therefore Joy is a desire for an object beyond the natural world and that object must exist.[6]

While Beversluis's argument contains all the needed premises, in order to simplify it, we should break it down to see all of its constituent parts:

1. All natural desires have existing objects that satisfy them.
2. Joy is a natural desire.
3. Therefore Joy has an existing object that satisfies it.

Consequently, the follow up to this argument would go as follows:

4. Joy has an existing object that satisfies it.
5. But the object of Joy is not found anywhere in this world.
6. Therefore the existing object of Joy is not of this world.

Notice that *if* the previous five premises are true then the final conclusion (number 6) is *necessarily* true. Everything in this argument hinges on two very fundamental points. The first is whether or not *all* natural

---

5. Lewis, *Regress*, 204–5.
6. Beversluis, *Lewis and Search*, 41.

desires have objects that exist to satisfy them. The second is whether or not Joy is really a natural desire that has nothing on earth to satisfy it. If a strong case can be made for these two points, then the conclusion that there must be something outside of this world that serves as Joy's object of satisfaction is strong as well. But even if we allow this deductive form of the argument, it still hinges on the inductive or abstract strength of the plausibility of the five previous premises themselves. This is not surprising. All deductive arguments are only as strong as the inductive or abstract strength of the premises that lead to their conclusions.[7] For example, even if we find that, by way of experience, the premise that "all men are mortal," is true, this does not have to mean it is a *necessary* truth. It only means that since we find that *all* humans have died (so far as history has shown), and that the nature of human beings is such that they have bodies that have physiological limitations that eventually lead to death, it is rational to universalize the statement that "all men are mortal." But if we were to find even one person that is immortal, this might well force us to remove the universal statement that asserted that "all" men were mortal. But no such person has been found to date and such a proposition is not consistent with all the known qualities of human bodies. So even if "all men are mortal" is not a necessary truth, it is a truth we find in our world nonetheless. Similarly, even if it is *possible* natural desires could exist without satisfying objects, this would not nullify the Argument from Desire *per se*. The Argument from Desire does not assert that all natural desires *necessarily* have objects that satisfy them. We can imagine a world where aliens constantly crave eating but, nonetheless, live off of something other than eating. As impractical as that might seem, it is certainly not a logical impossibility. But the point Lewis makes is that no such objectless natural desire has been found in human nature. Thus one may rationally universalize the first premise even if only in the Humean "matter of fact" sense.

Nevertheless, pretend *one* such natural desire that has no satisfying object *was* to be found. This would still not defeat the Argument from

---

7 An "abstract" concept can be gained by knowing something general about a thing. For example, knowing something about human beings generally speaking is to know something about them "abstractly." We do not have to know every human being to draw conclusions about human nature generally. We will get into why all this is important in the next chapter.

Desire *per se*. It would only bring us to its inductive form (we will save further discussion about why this issue is important in chapter 5).

Thus, either way one looks at it, even without the deductive version of the argument the inductive version still allows for a strong case for the Argument from Desire. Interestingly enough, after examining the material in *Mere Christianity* and *Weight of Glory*, Beversluis offers this inductive form that he finds there:

1. Many natural desires have objects that can satisfy them.
2. Joy is a natural desire for a kind of satisfaction that no object in the natural world can satisfy.
3. Therefore Joy is a desire for an object beyond the natural world and that object probably exists.[8]

Even allowing for this weaker inductive form of the argument, one would still be more warranted to affirm the conclusion than to deny it.

However, while Lewis used terms like "most probable" in presenting his conclusion, there is no indication that Lewis ever entertained the idea that there actually exists any innate desires that have no objects to satisfy them. Even in the case of the above quote from *Mere Christianity*, Lewis observes that "Creatures are not born with desires unless satisfaction for those desires exists." Clearly Lewis believed that *all* innate desires just so happen to have objects that satisfy them. Even if this truth is not a *logically necessary* truth, it is a truth that happens to exist within the world of human nature nonetheless.

The strength of the argument truly rests on what Lewis is saying here. This is why it is best to see the humble spirit in Lewis when he uses phrases like "most probable" and "pretty good indication" in offering his conclusions. Lewis recognized that there is no one argument that will serve to settle the matter for everyone. He also knew that there was no one formal argument that could prove with Cartesian certainty the truthfulness of the Christian faith. Any differences in the wording of Lewis's quotes on this subject can best be seen as simple rhetorical differences that spring from the nature and purpose of the work itself. This is supported by the fact that in *The Weight of Glory* he is expounding a sermon and in *Mere Christianity* he is being more practical in his tone. Yet in the Afterword of *The Pilgrim's Regress* Lewis offers a more analytical and

---

8. Beversluis, *Lewis and Search*, 43.

explicit way of arguing his case. As Kreeft observes, "The *Surprised by Joy* passages are not primarily intended to argue but to reveal. The book is not philosophy but autobiography. Yet an argument is hinted at. The passage in *Mere Christianity* is more argumentative than *Surprised by Joy*, but is more practical, a matter of pastoral guidance. Only in the work *The Pilgrim's Regress* did Lewis use it as an explicit argument."[9]

Settling on Peter Kreeft's Version of the Argument

In any case, as stated at the beginning of this chapter, the reasons for bringing out these different forms of the argument are not moot. The point in doing so will be made clearer as we later address the objections that are made concerning the Argument from Desire. But for our main purposes we present Peter Kreeft's three basic premises of the argument to serve as the basis for our discussion in what follows. Notice that if the first two premises are true, the conclusion must also be true. The argument is worded as follows:

1. The major premise of the argument is that *every natural or innate desire in us bespeaks a corresponding real object that can satisfy the desire.*
2. The minor premise is that *there exists in us a natural desire which nothing in time, nothing on earth, no creature, can satisfy.*
3. The conclusion is that *there exists something outside of time, earth, and creatures which can satisfy this desire* . . . This something is what many people call God and heaven.[10]

It is important to note that the first premise of the argument implies that there are at least two kinds of desires. This point is critical in understanding the argument. There are innate (i.e., natural and universal) desires and there are conditioned (i.e., artificial) ones. This premise does not say that if someone merely wishes something to be true it must be. Kreeft makes this distinction very clear when he writes, "We naturally desire things like food, drink, sex, knowledge, friendship, and beauty . . . We also desire things like Rolls Royces, political offices, flying through

---

9. Kreeft, *Heaven*, 206.
10. Ibid., 201–2. Italics mine.

the air like superman . . ."[11] This premise is explained more succinctly by Lewis in the quote given above from *Mere Christianity*. Lewis is speaking of the kind of desires that we are "born with." They are desires for such things as food, water, and sex.[12]

So if there are natural and universal desires, then there must be some reason we have them. As stated above, even from an evolutionary perspective a desire cannot survive long if it serves no purpose for survival. Even John Beversluis, who is a staunch critic of the Argument from Desire, believes that there is no evolutionary purpose for the kind of desire Lewis defended and yet we have the desire anyway.[13] If this is so, then the question here is, why do we have this natural divine desire at all? Again, we will discuss the evolutionary objection to the Argument from Desire in part 4.

With the risk of sounding redundant, it is important to emphasize, again, what Lewis is *not* saying. We do this because it is one of the most misunderstood aspects of his argument. He is *not* saying that the existence of *just any kind of desire* implies that the object of that desire exists. If I wish long and hard enough for unicorns to exist this will not prove that they do. This is what people mean by mere "wishful thinking." The major premise in the argument is specifically speaking of innate (i.e., universal and natural) desires. For example, hunger means that food of some kind exists, and thirst means that some kind of drink exists, and so forth.

Since the present work asserts that this first premise is so fundamental, further comments will be addressed in chapter 5 in part 2 when we deal with certain objections to the argument.

The second (minor) premise is the most interesting and yet also the most challenging. Because of this we will spend all of part 3 looking at existential and external hints that point us to the truth of this premise. This is where the role of Lewis's *Sehnsucht* becomes critical. According to Lewis all innate desires except one have a corresponding object that is identifiable and can be located in time and space. There exists in us, however, one natural desire that nothing in time or earth can satisfy. As discussed above, *Sehnsucht* is the German word that refers to this kind of longing. Yet, if one is open to it, one can see that we live in a world that is

---

11. Ibid., 202.
12. Lewis, *Mere Christianity*, 136.
13. Beversluis, *Lewis and Search*, 45.

filled with constant reminders of this otherworldly object. "The phenomenon the Germans call *Sehnsucht* is psychologically fascinating, and when it occurs as subject rather than thinking object—i.e., when we experience the desire rather than just thinking about it—it is obsessive and imperious—in fact, even more imperious than erotic desire at its height . . . for the object of *Sehnsucht* is the perfect heavenly beloved, whether we know it or not."[14]

It is *Sehnsucht* that makes people so religiously dedicated to the point where they are willing to lose everything for the sake of it. *Sehnsucht* is what moved the apostle Paul to write in Philippians 1:21–23: "For to me, to live is Christ, and to die is gain. But if I live on in the flesh, this will mean fruit from my labor; yet what I shall choose I cannot tell. For I am hard-pressed between the two, having a desire to depart and be with Christ, which is far better." Paul's longing, which produced a kind of aching for home, motivated him to know and to anticipate that there was something more after his earthly life was over.

The conclusion of the argument, therefore, claims that what we desire is not identifiable with anything on earth. It does not claim, by itself, to prove the existence of the Christian God. Nevertheless, as we will discuss in part 3, it is *rational* to affirm that this natural hunger and homesickness is a reliable source for believing in a supernatural place and being.

---

14. Kreeft, *Heaven*, 204.

PART 2

Examining Beversluis's Objections to the Argument

Introduction

LIKE ANY PHILOSOPHICAL ARGUMENT, the Argument from Desire does not come without its opponents. John Beversluis is one such opponent. In fact, he has written an entire volume dedicated to critiquing the apologetics of C. S. Lewis. In one of his chapters Beversluis challenged the Argument from Desire from a number of different angles. This part of the book will consider what Beversluis has to say about the argument. Our analysis will challenge his objections by showing that his criticisms are either without warrant or has missed the point of what C. S. Lewis was saying altogether. All of what Beversluis has to say about the argument will not be considered here due to the focus of this chapter. The discussion is limited to five key criticisms that are fundamental to the argument's success.

The first thing Beversluis seeks to do is to make a distinction between two forms of the argument found in Lewis's writings. He also responds to Robert Holyer's challenge to an earlier edition of Beversluis's book that addressed only the deductive form of the argument.[1] According to Holyer, Lewis posits only an inductive case for the argument (though he admits that Lewis himself "often speaks as though" one can argue it deductively).[2] But as we pointed out in the previous chapter, while we might be able to read Lewis offering an inductive case for the argument in works such as *Mere Christianity* and *Weight of Glory*, the Afterword to *The Pilgrim's Regress* seems to present a stronger, more deductive style of the argument. Beversluis is right to point this out, saying, "Robert Holyer thinks it is inductive and faults me for construing it as deductive. He seems not to have noticed that Lewis formulates it both ways."[3] Nevertheless, both Holyer and Kreeft have much to say to Beversluis's criticisms,

---

1. Beversluis, *Lewis and Search*, 40.
2. Holyer, "Argument," 68.
3. Beversluis, *Lewis and Search*, 40.

which will be pointed out in what follows, while offering our own analysis along the way.

The reader will note that there is one very important objection against the Argument from Desire that is not addressed here. The objection concerns the role evolution may have played in the formation of humanity's longing for God. We wait to deal with this objection in part 4 of this book. We do so for two reasons: 1) In part 2 we are only looking at Beversluis's objections in particular, and since he did not consider Lewis's idea of Joy to involve a *natural* desire, Beversluis did not discuss the evolutionary objection. 2) We also wait until part 4 of this book to deal with the evolutionary objection because it is in that section where we address the argument's conclusion. We thought it best to wait to discuss it until then simply because it applies more specifically to the concluding premise and to the very nature of the object which satisfies Lewis's desire. Consequently, the evolutionary objection can allow for premises 1 and 2 of the argument to be true and yet still deny the conclusion by asserting that humans have evolved brains that serve to create the illusion of God to satisfy these transcendent desires. Yet contrary to the evolutionary argument, all of Beversluis's objections deal primarily with either the first or second premise of the argument. Thus we deal with them separately in this book.

CHAPTER 5

Does Lewis "Beg The Question"?

IN ONE OF THE key objections Beversluis offers he wonders how Lewis could be in a position to know that all desires have objects to fill them if Joy is one such desire that is not filled (at least not in any of our current experiences). If there is even *one* exception, could there not be more? If there are more, then how many more? As Beversluis states,

> How could Lewis have known that every natural desire has an object that can satisfy it before he knew that Joy has one? . . . I can know that every natural desire has an object that can satisfy it only if I know that each of them has one individually. That is, the truth of the universal proposition "Every natural desire has an object that can satisfy it" is contingent on a host of particular propositions about particular natural desires whose truth must be discovered first.[1]

In other words, Beversluis claims that Lewis commits the fallacy of *petitio principii* (i.e., "begging the question"). How can you know that Joy has an object that can be satisfied if it has never been satisfied? And how can you say all desires have satisfying objects if we have not found an object to satisfy Joy?

Holyer's Response to Beversluis

Robert Holyer breaks down the argument in a way that helps us to see this objection better:

1. Ibid., 42–3.

1. All natural desires have existing objects that they are desires for.
2. Joy is a natural desire for an infinite object.
3. Therefore, an infinite object exists.[2]

Beversluis's objection really attacks the truth of the major premise above (1). This is where Holyer takes issue with the deductive form of the argument (as criticized by Beversluis) that makes the major premise a universal affirmative proposition. Again, in asking, "How could Lewis know that every natural desire has a real object before knowing that Joy has one?" he is, again, accusing Lewis of begging the question.

This may be one of the oddest challenges to the Argument from Desire. Peter Kreeft summarizes this objection by saying that it asks, "How can anyone know the truth that every natural desire has a real object without first knowing that this natural desire too has a real object?"[3] To put the objection simply, how could you make such a bold claim that "all" innate desires have objects to satisfy them when you claim that the innate desire Lewis speaks of is never satisfied (at least, not in this world)? If even one desire does not have an object that satisfies the desire, then does this not negate the universal term "all" in the premise, and thus, calling into question the whole argument? Because we already covered much of this in chapter 4 we will try to only say as much as is needed to be said in relation to Beversluis's objection.

Again, this objection is one reason why Holyer prefers the inductive approach. Holyer thinks Beversluis is right to criticize the deductive form of the argument. He claims that we could not know the major premise (1) unless we first knew the conclusion (3). According to Beversluis, we must first prove that the infinite object exists in order to know whether the first premise could be true. Thus, Holyer wants to remove the word "all" from the major premise. Holyer believes this argument is more successful in its inductive form. He suggests that since *most* natural desires that we experience have objects that satisfy them, it is *most probable* that the natural desire for God suggests that God exists too. Holyer's way of seeing this is interesting, and, as we stated in chapter 4, it could still show the argument to be compelling. But is there another way of answering Beversluis's objection?

2. Holyer, "Argument," 68.
3. Kreeft, *Heaven*, 226.

Does the Deductive Form of the Argument Really Beg the Question?

Even assuming the deductive argument, does Beversluis's objection really work? On the surface it might seem so. But a careful analysis will show that it ultimately fails to offer any reliable defeater to the argument.

First, Beversluis blinds himself by his own empiricist commitments. He seems to assume that we must be able to know about *every possible* object that exists in the world before we can conclude that Joy is not satisfied by anything on earth. But, as Kreeft rightly affirms, this objection "amounts to saying that only through sense experience and induction is any knowledge possible, that there is only *a posteriori* knowledge, no *a priori* knowledge. This is Positivism, or at least, Empiricism."[4]

To build on what we said in chapter 4, in order to answer Beversluis's objection here, the only thing that must be done is to demonstrate that one can know universal truths concerning innate desires and the objects that fulfill them without the need to have exhaustive knowledge of *every possible* desire and its specific correlating object. Peter Kreeft gives us an account of such a way of knowing, saying, "We can and do come to a knowledge of universals through abstraction, not only by induction. For example we know that all men must be mortal, or capable of speech, or laughter, or prayer, not in the same way that we know that all men have non-green skin, by mere sense observation, but by understanding something about human nature, which we meet in, and abstract from, the individuals we experience."[5]

Beversluis does respond to this statement by Kreeft. But, surprisingly, the only comment Beversluis makes about this is that Kreeft merely gets this idea from the "Aristotelian-Thomistic" tradition which "few contemporary philosophers" find "plausible."[6] Hence, Beversluis asserts, "It cannot be introduced into the discussion without argument, uncritically assumed to be true, and used as a basis for his entire argument."[7] What is a bit unfair about this statement is that Kreeft actually spends three pages offering an argument defending his position.

---

4. Ibid., 226.
5. Ibid., 227.
6. Beversluis, *Lewis and Search*, 56.
7. Ibid.

Beversluis commits at least two fallacies here. The first fallacy Beversluis commits is the *genetic fallacy*. A genetic fallacy occurs when an opponent of an argument claims he has disproven the argument by attacking the source of the argument rather than the content of the argument itself. Beversluis does this when he implies that Kreeft's position should not be taken seriously because it comes from an "Aristotelian-Thomistic" tradition. The second fallacy he commits is the *ad populum* fallacy (i.e., appealing to the majority). Even if we grant Beversluis's assertion, just because "few contemporary philosophers" do not find the "Aristotelian-Thomistic thesis" plausible still should not bias the reader against Kreeft's position. But Beversluis is not at all shy to use such emotional appeals and genetic fallacies in his arguments.

On another occasion he speaks of the Argument from Desire as "not only unoriginal, it is also suffocatingly Western and ethnocentric."[8] What exactly does Beversluis mean by "suffocatingly Western"? One wonders if the argument would still be "suffocating" if it were an Eastern idea. Again, instead of attacking the substance of Lewis's argument, he attacks what he views as the source of the argument.

Yet the worst part of this objection is shown in the fact that, if accepted, it really calls into question all forms of deductive reasoning. Consider the following classic example of a deductive syllogism:

1. All men are mortal.
2. Socrates is a man.
3. Therefore Socrates is a mortal.

Yet if we adopt Beversluis's objection to the Argument from Desire, then we will have to object to this argument as well. Remember that Beversluis believes that one cannot know the truth of the major premise (which says that all innate desires have existing objects that satisfy them) without first knowing the truth-value of the conclusion that the desire of Joy must have an object which satisfies it. But let's use this objection against the Socrates illustration. Is one to think that there is no way we could even know if "all" men are mortal (1) until we first know whether or not Socrates is a mortal (3)? Just because every other human being has been mortal until Socrates does not rule out that perhaps (while he was alive) Socrates was thought to be the sole exception. Now that he is dead

8. Ibid., 53.

Does Lewis "Beg The Question"?

we might just put anyone else living today in that minor premise and conclusion. In fact, how does anyone alive today know for certain that they are, in fact, mortal? According to Beversluis, without first proving that every individual person is mortal (3) one will never be able to generalize whether or not *all* men are indeed mortal (1).

Of course, unless one is a skeptical empiricist, no one consistently or instinctively reasons the way Beversluis does here. Again, it may be true that a man might not *necessarily* be a mortal. As mentioned in the previous chapter, we can imagine a possible world (maybe even our own?) where an exception could be made. But such would only imply a supernatural (or, if you like, "extraordinary") cause for this exception and Beversluis does not sound prepared to accept this.

Nevertheless, even if we look at this inductively, Beversluis's objection is still shown to be weak. For example, we do not have to know every human being in order to rationally conclude that *this* particular human being (call him X) will die. If, in every case we have experienced so far, all humans have died, then we are warranted to draw the conclusion, naturally speaking, that person X will die.

In the same way, if we see that all innate desires (such as hunger, sex, and thirst) have some object that satisfies them, then we are warranted to conclude that the natural desire for the divine has an object that satisfies it as well. While not putting it exactly in this way, this is one reason Holyer prefers the inductive approach to the argument. In his view, one can demonstrate, even if not necessarily, that the innate desire for a transcendent being strongly suggests that it (what we might call God) exists.

Chapter 6

Does The Quality of *Sehnsucht* Lack "Innateness"?

JOHN BEVERSLUIS OFFERS ANOTHER objection that simply denies that Lewis is able to say that desire for God is a natural (or innate) one. He wonders how one can speak of Joy as being a natural desire when all natural desires are only produced out of a need for survival and Joy (per Beversluis) simply cannot fit this category.

He rightly says that, "A desire that is not innate does not arise spontaneously in all physiological and psychological normal organisms, but is culturally or societally induced."[1] Thus some desires are natural (such as hunger) but some desires are artificial (such as wanting to drive a Mercedes). According to Beversluis, Lewis's idea of Joy is not something that arises spontaneously in all people. It is more like wanting to drive a Mercedes. To further explain what he means by "natural desire," Beversluis offers this inquiry: "What does Lewis mean by natural desire? He offers no definition or explanation, but his examples suggest that he means an innate desire that arises spontaneously in all physiologically and psychologically normal human beings . . . and is traceable to, and partly constitutive of, the nature of the human . . . organisms that experience it."[2]

He then goes on to offer his own definition of what a natural desire is: "Natural desires are biological and instinctive—evolutionary adaptations that trigger appropriate responses to external stimuli and whose satisfaction is necessary for the survival of individual organisms of the species of which they are member."[3]

1. Beversluis, *Lewis and Search*, 45.
2. Ibid.
3. Ibid.

Beversluis concludes from this that "Joy is not a natural desire" because "it is not an evolutionary adaptation to external stimuli. And satisfaction of it is not necessary for the survival of the organisms that experience it."[4]

Challenging Beversluis's Materialistic Assumptions

For the most part I think Lewis might agree that natural desires are "biological and instinctive." However, the claim that the only reason we have natural desires is that they arise strictly from a need for survival would be an assumption Lewis would not accept. Beversluis seems to be arguing:

1. A natural desire is only that which arises from appropriate responses to external stimuli whose satisfaction is needed for survival.
2. Joy is not a desire that arises from appropriate responses to external stimuli whose satisfaction is needed for survival (i.e., we do not need it to survive).
3. Therefore Joy is not a natural desire.

But Beversluis begs the question in the first (i.e., major) premise in that he *assumes* a strict materialist model of natural selection. In other words, by saying that natural desires can only be formed because of some natural necessity for survival he is setting up *secular* and *arbitrary* rules for determining whether or not there can be a supernatural origin for any innate desires we may have. Beversluis needs to assume this materialist model of natural selection in order to determine what a person can or cannot possess innately because if he allows for anything else his whole objection crumbles. If supernatural creation is at all even *possible* then some innate desires might exist for some other reason besides mere biological survival. Beversluis seems to ignore the fact that human beings seek to flourish not just survive. Humans have psychological and spiritual desires that have nothing to do with mere survival.

The Possibility of Supernaturally Designed Desires

One may question the legitimacy of Beversluis's first premise by simply denying it and suggesting that some of our innate desires are explained by

4. Ibid.

divine creation. If so, then human mental faculties can arise out of more than just a simple need to survive and Joy could very well be one of them. Thus, the need for survival is not necessarily the only possible source for natural human desires. Again, Beversluis's objection is valid only if we assume that there is no creative design and that the necessity for survival is the only source for all our existing human faculties and desires. But Beversluis does not prove this assumption.

Once again, Beversluis ties his own hands with his empiricism. As with the first objection, Beversluis's claims imply that the only way to knowledge is through sense experience. We could grant that Joy is not an evolutionary adaptation to "external stimuli" for the survival of the human species, but that still does not mean it is not natural and innate. The real evidence for Joy's innateness does not come through Beversluis's self-imposed biological empiricist criteria. It comes as a result of looking at the way the rational world works via *a priori* as well as *a posteriori* realities. This involves a combination of human introspection and environmental, social, and biological analysis. Contrary to Beversluis, we do not deny the biological elements behind the experience of Lewis's concept of Joy (see part 4 for more on this). Rather what is denied here is that this biological element can come *only* through an "adaptation to external stimuli for human survival." To the contrary, we are here affirming that there can be such a thing as an essential human *nature* that is *divinely designed* that may exist before any experience arises at all in life. We also affirm that C. S. Lewis's concept of Joy as intense (albeit non-coercive) divine longing is included in this essential nature. Beversluis, of course, denies this.

Consequently, unlike the atheistic existentialist worldview, we believe that humanity possesses a divinely intended *essence* even before any particular person comes into *existence*.[5] This means that there is a divine *telos* about *human nature* that serves as a paradigm before an individual comes into the world. Once we are conceived, we do not come into this world as "blank slates." Recall again part of Beversluis's definition when

5. A claim that is contrary to the Secular Existentialists who have asserted that humanity's *existence* precedes everything about their *essence*. Human beings, according to this worldview, are *only* defined by what they make of themselves. What it means to be a human being is entirely dependent upon the existing individual person. This claim runs counter to the Judeo-Christian view that says that God created human beings "after his own image" (Gen 1:26–27). In this view, God has a pre-existing design for what a human being is (and is *supposed*) to be.

he said that "natural desires" are "evolutionary adaptations that trigger appropriate responses to external stimuli." But if there is a God who made us, then it stands to reason that he designed us with certain faculties that are intended to interact with our world in a certain way (i.e., before any external stimuli produces it). It is as Mary Midgley once said: "Sensible psychologists have accordingly tended more and more to admit that people do have some genetically fixed tendencies."[6] In this way, the tendency toward Joy can be viewed as innate (i.e., *a priori*). This does not mean it does not have an experiential (i.e., *a posteriori*) element to it. But this experiential role is not as much adaptive (eg. for survival) as it is suggestive (i.e., serving to point us to something else). Thus, humanity's biological tendencies toward Joy, working together with our experiences of life, tend to move us further along in our divine search, the way Lewis chronicles his own search in *Surprised by Joy*. And since one can see this kind of search in all cultures throughout all human history, this just adds to the strength of Lewis's argument.

So contrary to Beversluis's claim, Joy is not like wanting to drive a Mercedes. It works more like the desire to eat a lunch that is not being offered yet. But there will be more to say about the evidence for this in chapters 14–15.

---

6. Midgley, *Beast and Man*, 19.

Chapter 7

If "Joy" Is So Natural and Desirable, Then Why Did Lewis Run Away from It?

ANOTHER OBJECTION BEVERSLUIS OFFERS is that if a desire for God is something humans tend to move naturally *toward*, then why did C. S. Lewis, according to his own words, want to run away from it when he felt it? In fact, Lewis spoke of a kind of a "terror" that came over him at certain times whenever he felt this Joy. In *Surprised by Joy* he pondered this in his quest: "For all I knew the total rejection of what I called Joy might be one of the demands, might be the first demand, He would make upon me. There was no strain of music from within, no smell of eternal orchards at the threshold, when I was dragged through the doorway. No kind of desire was present at all."[1]

Consequently, Beversluis wonders, "If God is really Joy's ultimate object, and if all desire is ultimately desire for him, why, when Lewis was brought face to face with him, did he cease to desire him and search for a way of escape?"[2]

The Often Sporadic and Ambiguous Nature of "Joy"

Beversluis's critical issue here is why there was such an ambiguity within Lewis if Joy is what his heart always longed for. While on the surface this objection might sound compelling, in many ways, it is really one of the easier ones to answer.

While we will say more about this subject further below, we first point out here that, according to Lewis, the unsatisfied longing for which

1. Lewis, *Surprised*, 230–31.
2. Beversluis, *Lewis and Search*, 56.

If "Joy" Is So Natural and Desirable, Then Why Did Lewis Run Away from It?

"nothing on earth can satisfy" is not something that is obviously or immediately identified. Neither is it a sense that is always felt in life. In *Surprised by Joy* Lewis said that there were only three occasions that he could remember as a youth feeling this kind of "intense transcendent desire."

The first occasion was when he was standing beside a "flowering current bush on a summer day."[3] Lewis describes how, without warning, he remembered the time in his old house when his brother had brought a toy garden into the nursery. There was something in the beauty of that garden that solicited a feeling unknown to Lewis before then. This is how he describes the memory:

> It is difficult to find words strong enough for the sensation which came over me; Milton's "enormous bliss" of Eden (giving the full, ancient meaning to "enormous") comes somewhere near it. It was a sensation, of course, of desire; but desire for what? Not, certainly, for a biscuit tin filled with moss, nor even (though that came into it) for my past . . . and before I knew it the desire was gone, the whole glimpse withdrawn, the world turned commonplace again, or only stirred by a longing for the longing that had just ceased. It had taken only a moment of time; and in a sense everything else that had ever happened to me was insignificant in comparison.[4]

The second time Lewis felt this experience was in the reading of a book entitled *The Tale of Squirrel Nutkin* by Beatrix Potter. This is a children's book about a red squirrel named Nutkin who escapes from an owl named Old Brown. During his reading Lewis had an overwhelming feeling of what he calls the "Idea of Autumn." To have such a strong feeling for a season of the year, Lewis admits, "sounds fantastic." Why should autumn give such an "intense desire" for something beyond itself? Whatever it was, Lewis says, "It was something quite different from ordinary life and even from ordinary pleasure; something, as they would now say, 'in another dimension.'"[5]

The third time Lewis remembers feeling this transcendent longing as a youth was while reading a poem. During his reading one day he found himself, "Instantly uplifted into huge regions of northern sky, I desired with almost sickening intensity something never to be described . . . and

---

3. Lewis, *Surprised*, 15.
4. Ibid.
5. Ibid., 17.

then, as in the other examples, found myself at the very same moment already falling out of that desire and wishing I were back in it."[6]

These examples show that the desire for transcendence is not a twenty-four hour experience imposing itself upon us. Most of life is mundane and ordinary. But, as Lewis's autobiographical narratives show, *Sehnsucht* touches us during the deep (and often unexpected) moments in our lives.

But even when we get this feeling, according the Lewis, it is something that can commonly be misunderstood or mistaken for something else. As he states, "I had asked if Joy itself was what I wanted; and, labeling it 'aesthetic experience,' had pretended that I could answer Yes. But that too had broken down." This tendency to mistake Joy for aesthetic experience is due, in part, to the invisibility and mystery of the true object of our longing. As Lewis continues to say, "Far more objective than bodies, for it is not like them, clothed in our senses; the naked Other, imageless (though our imagination salutes it with a hundred images), unknown, undefined, desired."[7]

This is one reason this mysterious longing can also be described as an "aching" or "painful" experience. It is a yearning feeling one has and wants to continue having after the feeling has been lost. But just when it comes and draws your excitement and curiosity, it goes away and the normalcy of life is all that remains.

Why Lewis Ran Away

It was only later when Lewis started identifying what the object of the desire was that he began to fight against it. As Lewis himself attests to, "I had always wanted, above all things, not to be interfered with. I had wanted (mad wish) 'to call my soul my own.' I had been far more anxious to avoid suffering than to achieve delight . . . But now what had been an ideal became a command . . . Total surrender, the absolute leap in the dark, were demanded."[8]

A person understands this sense of ambiguity and struggle when they are in a relationship with a loved one. That loved one may be the greatest love of his/her life. But he/she will still have mixed feelings

6. Ibid.
7. Ibid., 221.
8. Ibid., 228.

toward the loved one at different times in life. They will still argue and there may still be tensions within any given relationship. This tension can arise especially when one realizes the great moral responsibility that comes with this "Desire" for the divine that Lewis speaks about. There are uncomfortable sacrifices that must be made when one confronts the "Object" of divine desire, and this was one of the big reasons for Lewis's reservation.

The problem for Lewis was not the Joy itself. It was his pride and fears getting in the way. As long as Joy stayed within the realm of aesthetics, everything was fine. But when confronted with the true object of Joy, Lewis hesitated. The Joy Lewis spoke of is filled with emotions. It carries a sense of longing, happiness, frustration, fear, anger, and hope. All of these emotions and experiences come from either our own internal struggles or the fact that we are living apart from the very object of our desire.

All of this gets to the heart of Beversluis's current objection. Beversluis seems to expect that Joy, as Lewis describes it, should be coercive. He seems to forget that along with this positive sense of desired "longing" there also comes a responsibility and sacrifice that many do not wish to have in their lives. But Joy, when felt, does not remove a person's freedom. Like Kreeft says, "Everyone knows that we often love and hate, desire, and fear, the same object at different times or even at the same time, especially if that object is a person."[9] But we will have more to say about this point in response to Beversluis's fifth objection. But before leaving this objection, we will illustrate our response to it with a very pertinent scene in Lewis's *The Last Battle*.

On Avoiding False Beliefs and Failing to See the Truth at the Same Time

Sometimes in our attempt to avoid being naive we fall into the other extreme of being overly cynical. This was the error of the Dwarfs in *The Last Battle* of Lewis's Chronicles of Narnia. In the scene where King Tirian had revealed the truth that Puzzle (the donkey) was not really Aslan, the Dwarfs became mystified at how they could have been so easily fooled. Because of this previous deception, they vowed never to allow themselves to believe in Aslan. They figured that if they could be "taken in" once, they

---

9. Kreeft, *Heaven*, 230.

could be taken in again.[10] So they, in a sense, ran away from the true Aslan in the same way that Lewis ran away from the true object of Joy.

The Narnian Dwarfs shut out their search for Aslan because they did not want to be bothered by foolish lies and inconvenient truths. They had closed their minds to anything and anyone other than themselves. While speaking to King Tirian, one of the Dwarfs named Griffle explained: "I don't think we want any more Kings—if you *are* Tirian, which you don't look like him—no more than we want any Aslans. We're going to look out for ourselves from now on and touch our caps to nobody. See?" Griffle's fellow Dwarfs agreed, saying, "That's right . . . We're on our own now. No more Aslan, no more Kings, no more silly stories about other worlds. The Dwarfs are for the Dwarfs."[11] Thus, the Dwarfs were so bent on rejecting error that they failed to see the truth in front of them. The moral of the story seems to be that this is why some unbelievers are unbelievers. Some people become so fearful of being naive that they run toward blind cynicism. This is why, for a while at least, Lewis ran away from Joy. In similar words borrowed from the Narnian Dwarfs, "Lewis was for Lewis." His longing for the divine became, for him, an inconvenient truth until he came to the realization that this object of Joy was what he was always made for—what he really wanted the whole time but just refused to see or admit.

---

10. Lewis, *Last Battle*, 707.
11. Ibid.

CHAPTER 8

Does the Concept of *Sehnsucht* Contradict the Bible?

THIS FOURTH OBJECTION FROM Beversluis comes from his understanding of the Bible and how it relates to what Lewis says about Joy. Thus, Beversluis's objections are not "only on logical grounds but on theological grounds as well."[1] Therefore it is appropriate at this point to examine whether the Bible says anything at all about what Lewis calls Joy.

Beversluis boldly asserts that the "concept of God as the universal object of desire derives not from the Old or New Testament, but from Plato; and the Biblical texts that contradict it are legion."[2] But if there are legions of biblical texts it would have been nice for Beversluis to have offered one. It is in this writer's view that, instead of contradicting Lewis, the Bible offers many passages in favor of what he calls Joy. Of course, if Beversluis is looking for a place in the Bible that uses the word Joy the way Lewis uses it, he will not find one. But, again, the concept is found in many texts. Incidentally, people create many words that are not explicitly found in the Bible but which intend to communicate a concept that is there. Consider the word "trinity." The word is not found in the Bible even though it can be argued that the concept is.

Beversluis later makes a similar remark, saying, "We look in vain for a biblical counterpart to 'Joy.' According to the psalmist, what God requires is not a diligent searcher but a contrite and broken heart (Ps 34:18, 51:17)."[3] One wonders if Beversluis has ever read Hebrews 11:6, which

---

1. Beversluis, *Lewis and Search*, 64.
2. Ibid., 64.
3. Ibid.

says that God is a "rewarder of those who *diligently seek* Him."[4] Beversluis would also have done well to reference Paul's sermon on Mars Hill where Paul affirms that God made us in order that we would "*seek* Him" (Acts 17:26–27).[5] There will be more to say about this passage below.

The Importance of Acknowledging the Audience of the Biblical Texts

As far as humanity's desire for God goes, we submit that this idea is found throughout the biblical record. Believers are found everywhere proclaiming praises like "As the deer pants for water brooks, so pants my soul for You, O God. My soul thirsts for God, for the living God . . . My tears have been food day and night, while they continually say 'Where is your God?'" (Ps 42:1–3; 63:1). Additionally, we find this desire in the famous Beatitudes when Jesus proclaimed, "Blessed are those who hunger and thirst for righteousness" (Matt 5:6).

But it might well be objected that verses like these are written by those who already believe. These verses, it may be asserted, do not support the idea that mankind's desire for God is an innate or natural one. In order to answer Beversluis's objection we will need to find additional evidence that unbelievers are "haunted" by this unquenchable hunger for the transcendence that Lewis wrote about.

This poses an interesting challenge. One hopes that Beversluis would not expect to find very many passages that support what Lewis called Joy because biblical texts were written to audiences that were already believers. In fact, there is very little evidence for much of what we would call strict "atheism" in the ancient world. There must be a reason for this. On one hand, some elitist atheists might be tempted to say that people in the ancient world simply were not educated enough to be pure atheists. On the other hand, one also might argue that the modern formal educational system that has sprung from the Enlightenment has produced many materialists who have bought the lie that human beings can figure everything out by themselves. But whatever else might be said, it is certainly possible that atheism in the ancient world was rarer, in part, because they lacked the many modern academic and social pressures that can serve

---

4. Italics mine.
5. Italics mine.

as barriers to the human inclination toward faith that we have today.[6] It is not argued here that this is the only reason for atheism. What is being argued is that this may account for its institutional and social growth in the modern era. This is certainly a different perspective from those who argue that the rise of atheism is primarily due to the progress of scientific knowledge of the world.

Be that as it may, the point here is that finding very many verses in the Bible that address the subject of atheism will be rare and difficult. Nevertheless, one does find hints at Joy in the Bible as it relates to mans search for God. Let us offer just two examples below.

Biblical Evidence for Man's Natural Desire for God

First, we find in the book of Ecclesiastes a writer that legitimately tried to find the answer to the meaning of life without theological assumptions. While he may have been a believer in God, he still seems to have genuinely tried to find satisfaction in life without him. Notice, "I set my heart to seek and search out by wisdom concerning all that is done under heaven; this burdensome task God has given to the sons of man, by which they may be afflicted. I have seen all the works that are done under the sun; and indeed, all is vanity and grasping for the wind" (Eccl 1:13–14).

The phrase "under the sun" refers to the author's search for meaning within a secular point of view (i.e., looking for meaning in the world without theological considerations). No matter where he tried to find it, he could only find vanity. The desire of his heart could not be filled by the many avenues he sought.[7] Notice also the theme of "grief" and "sorrow" that comes with this longing,

> What is crooked cannot be made straight, and what is lacking cannot be numbered. I communed with my heart, saying, "Look, I have attained greatness, and have gained more wisdom than all who were before me in Jerusalem. My heart has understood great wisdom and knowledge." And I set my heart to know wisdom and to know madness and folly. I perceived that this also is grasping for

---

6. One needs to look no further than to watch Ben Stein's documentary titled *Expelled: No Intelligence Allowed* to see the impact that social and academic pressures have had on public faith in the West.

7. See part one for more on this point as it relates to Ecclesiastes.

the wind. For in much wisdom *is* much grief, and he who increases knowledge increases sorrow. (Eccl 1:15–18.)

The "sorrow" that is felt from the aching of an unsatisfied desire is reminiscent of the motif found in *Sehnsucht*. While we will not take the time and space to address the issues here, Beversluis would do well to consider more of what Ecclesiastes has to say about these themes.

Second, we find in Acts 17 something that bears a likeness to *Sehnsucht*. The apostle Paul is preaching to a group of philosophers who were diverse in their views, with some of them holding to views that would be considered agnostic, at least, in some sense (i.e., certain Stoic and Epicurean philosophers). But some of the Athenians worshipped an "unknown god" just in case there was something else out there that they had missed (Acts 17:23). This point is telling in itself. Among all the objects that they were looking for to fill their desire for transcendence, they believed there was possibly something "more," something yet "unknown." Nothing they worshipped led them to think that what they had identified so far sufficiently satisfied their craving for God. If any place could have satisfied a person's longing for transcendence it should have been Athens.

Thus Paul preached to them this "unknown" God that they sought to worship. Paul believed that the God he served was the God who would eventually give them the satisfaction they were craving. Travelers were coming from all over the world to Athens to hear some "new thing" (17:21). People are always looking for "new things" because they always sense that they need more: more beauty, more aesthetic feelings, more pleasure, more happiness, more answers, more everything. When Paul preached a resurrected Jesus many of them apparently believed they had finally found the "new thing" they were looking for (17:34).

What exactly was in Paul's message that brought many of them to convert? Part of it must have been his point found in verses 26–29. Paul makes an incredible point that God created humanity for the very reason that they "should seek the Lord, in hope that they might grope for Him and find Him, though He is not far from each one of us. For in Him we live and move and have our being, as also some of your own poets have said, 'For we are also His offspring.' Therefore since we are his offspring, we ought not to think that the Divine Nature is like gold or silver or stone, something shaped by man's hands."

There are three points from this text that are important for our purposes here:

First, Paul said that God made us to "seek," "grope," and "find Him." The word "grope" comes from the Greek word meaning to "touch" or "feel."[8] Obviously this cannot mean that we are supposed to be walking around trying to feel God with our hands. It has a metaphorical use implying that God has created us with the ability to begin *finding* him by *feeling* our way toward him. We must remember that he says this to a Roman audience who may likely never have seen copies of Israel's canonical texts. Clearly Paul is suggesting something like what is related to Lewis's use of Joy (or transcendent desire). This idea of feeling our way around is reminiscent of Lewis's autobiographical account of his own search in *Surprised by Joy*.

Second, Paul argues that even pagan poets know we are, at least in some sense, made in the "image of God" (17:28–29). Paul testifies that even, "some of your own poets have said, 'For we are also His offspring'" (17:28). More than likely Paul is alluding to the poet Aratus who believed that all people were the offspring of Zeus. But Paul is not arguing at this point which God was the right one. He was arguing simply that we all have some intuition or feeling that we come from something higher than just our parents or anything else in *this* world. Paul believed we could get this without studying the Bible. This gets to the second premise of the Argument from Desire, which we will further elaborate on later.

Third, Paul teaches that our natural world should point us to a supernatural object. Paul said, "Since we are the offspring of God, we ought not to think that the Divine Nature is like gold or silver or stone, something shaped by art and man's devising" (17:29). This verse also alludes to the second premise of the Argument from Desire. Nature suggests to us that there is no earthly object that will satisfy the transcendent sense that is within us. According to Paul, the divine object must be something unlike "gold, or silver or stone, something shaped by art and man's devising" (17:29). Paul affirmed something similar to this in Romans 1:20.

Thus, it seems that Beversluis misses much of what the Bible says that is consistent with Lewis's Argument from Desire.

---

8. Thayer, *Lexicon*, 676.

CHAPTER 9

Why Do Some People Never Experience What C. S. Lewis Calls "Joy"?

WE NOW COME TO what is believed by some to be the most compelling of all the objections put forth by Beversluis. He asks, "What about people who have no interest in or are indifferent to nature, music, and literature? What about people who have no idea what you are talking about when you try to explain Joy to them? What about severely mentally handicapped or autistic people?"[1] Later he asks again, how can we "account for those people who cannot find the desire within?"[2] Why, if Lewis's desire is so innate or universal, do we find so many people who do not desire what Lewis came to desire in *Surprised by Joy*? This is the kind of person who says, "I simply do not observe any such desire for God, or heaven, or infinite joy, or some mysterious x which is more than any earthly happiness."[3] Thus, if Lewis is correct, how then do we account for atheism in the world?

This objection is similar to the objection we dealt with in chapter 7. The main difference is that chapter 7 dealt with why Lewis ran away from Joy *when he experienced it*. The objection we are now confronted with deals with those who deny they have ever felt it *at all*.

According to Kreeft this denial can take two forms. One person can just admit that they may not be perfectly content with life right now but that they would be "if only" they had a million dollars, or a better spouse, or an immortality pill. The simple response to this person is that in the history of the world no one has ever found that one satisfying object that made him/her say, "I need nothing else in my life anymore." There will

---

1. Beversluis, *Lewis and Search*, 53.
2. Ibid., 55.
3. Kreeft, *Heaven*, 225.

always be "just one more thing" needed to make us happy, even if we are not quite sure what that one thing is. For this person we could just say, along with Peter Kreeft, "Try it. You won't like it. Billions of people have performed trillions of 'if only' experiments with life and they all had the same result: failure."[4] As noted earlier,[5] the writer of the book of Ecclesiastes tried all sorts of "what if" experiments that failed for him too.

The second way someone could deny he/she has ever felt Joy as Lewis described it is simply to say that he/she is completely satisfied with life. The person does not say, "I would only be happy if . . ." but rather, "I am perfectly content now."[6] For Kreeft, this person "verges" on "culpable dishonesty." For some, perhaps Kreeft is correct. However, there are many honest people who think that they are completely happy and lack nothing at all, even without anything like God. What can be said to these people if the desire for God is supposed to be so natural? A possible response is as Kreeft suggests and what John Stuart Mill states, "It is better to be Socrates dissatisfied than a pig satisfied."[7] Some people have learned simply to be satisfied with the "mud" in life and have ignored *Sehnsucht* long enough to be numb to its urgings. To borrow from the words of Paul to Timothy, their consciences have become "seared" as with a hot iron (2 Tim 4:2). Just as it is difficult to feel with deadened nerves, so can it be difficult to have Joy with a lost sense of awe about the world. If, as Beversluis says, some people "have no interest in or are indifferent to nature, music, and literature," then maybe they have misplaced more than *Sehnsucht*. To be "indifferent to nature" is to have lost what it means to live life as a human being at all. Beversluis's objection does not prove that there is no *Sehnsucht* in the human being. Again, given their indifference to life, it better proves that there are people who have learned to avoid divine Joy, and have pushed out of their active consciousness their natural longing to flourish as human beings.

But while these are practical answers that do make sense and may satisfy some, they may still not be enough for others. Can we say more for those who, like Beversluis, are just convinced that they have never felt this longing for God and eternal life? I think we can say a bit more.

4. Ibid., 225.
5. See pgs. 14–15 above.
6. Ibid.
7. Ibid.

The Non-coercive Nature of Man's Desire for God

In short, Beversluis's objection finds its answers in three very important points that are different and yet in many respects related to each other. First, whatever desires God may instill in us, they are not coercive. Just because something may be natural does not mean it must always be inevitable. As long as their cognitive faculties are working properly, human beings will have free will. This freedom also includes the ability to control or even starve our natural instincts (think of the person on a starvation diet who, after so long, stops feeling the hunger pangs). Second, the Christian can contend that humans live in a fallen world where the sense of the divine has become blurred through pride, fear, and rebellion. Thus one may merely attribute the human desire for transcendence to a misplaced or exaggerated longing for some earthly thing or person. But again, as the Argument from Desire suggests, the natural and universal desire for transcendence must point to a real transcendent object (or subject). To repeat the first premise of the argument above: Every innate desire has a real object that exists to satisfy the desire. Thus a person might try to find an object besides food to satisfy his/her hunger, but this does not prove that food does not exist. In fact, what the person will find, even if too late, is that what he/she sought to satisfy his/her hunger was never sufficient to do the job. The person's search for satisfaction was misplaced. Pride, fear, and rebellion often point people to misplaced objects in life that never satisfy their human desire for transcendence. And third, God hides. According to the Christian perspective, God has created a world in which he chooses, at least in some sense, to hide his face. As Pascal noted, "God is a hidden God, and that since nature was corrupted, He has left men to their blindness, from which they can escape only through Jesus Christ."[8] Consequently, God is close enough for us to choose to find him, yet just far enough to allow us to choose not to. Paul expressed this in Acts 17 while preaching on Mars Hill saying, "And He has made from one blood every nation of men to dwell on all the face of the earth, and has determined their preappointed times and the boundaries of their dwellings, so that they should seek the Lord, in the hope that they might grope for Him and find Him, though He is not far from each one of us." (Acts 17:26–27)

While we looked at this passage above, we mention only that Paul taught that God "appointed our dwellings" in order that we would "seek"

---

8. Kreeft, *Christianity*, 251.

him and "grope" for him, even though he is not far from us. Again, Paul is telling this to people who do not have Bibles in their hands. Yet, according to Paul, God allows human beings this *sense* of absence in order to give us the gift of living and choosing freely. But to ensure humanity has no disadvantage, God has also given us these natural transcendent echoes (e.g., "hauntings" according to Otto; *sensus divinitatis* according to Aquinas and Plantinga; or *Sehnsucht* according to Lewis) to know that he is not far from us.

If all this is so, then we will always be at liberty, both to neglect this divine hunger, or to convince ourselves it has another object to which the hunger correlates. Thus, as Lewis stated in *The Great Divorce*, "There are only two kinds of people in the end: those who say to God, 'Thy will be done,' and those to whom God says 'Thy will be done.'"[9]

Clifford Williams wrote a book defending an existential case for the existence of God, in which he wrote,

> With these ideas in mind, we see that Lewis is asking us to notice what we have not noticed very well—the times when, for a fleeting moment, we have a faint sense of being haunted. We have not known exactly what by, and we have been too preoccupied to try to find out. But when we set aside our preoccupation and focus on the haunting perception, we see that it consists of a faint but nevertheless real desire for heaven—not all of heaven, perhaps, but at least some definite feature of it . . . Unfortunately, there are obstacles to making faint desires come to life.[10]

Cognitive and Emotional Obstacles to Faith

According to Williams there can be both cognitive and emotional obstacles to our inner desire for God. Most of the time people are not consciously aware of these obstacles. Some of the obstacles Williams mentions are anxiety, self-preoccupation, pride, and guilt. These and other factors can put up a "resistance" to the needs we have, so as to make people unaware that they even have them. He goes on to say, "These points about resistance and blindness explain why some people do not feel the need to be connected to anything divine or do not acknowledge feeling the need. It is

---

9. Lewis, *Divorce*, 73
10. Williams, *Reasons*, 114–15.

because they resist doing so."[11] He posits three basic ways one can remove this resistance: honesty, awareness, and/or willingness. These, according to Williams, are key ideas for how we can remove any resistance to the needs that motivate us toward the search for God. One example he gives is the need for divine forgiveness. "If for example, we have an inflated sense of self-importance, we will not be likely to feel a need to be forgiven by God. But if this inflamed sense is punctured, we become open to the need and thus are more likely to feel it."[12]

Williams offers an analogy to further explain why some people do not consciously feel certain natural needs that exist in their lives.

> My response to the "not everyone" objection can be illustrated by an ordinary psychological case. Let us look at the emotional hermit again, the one who insulates himself from his feelings and emotions. He does not easily reveal them to others, nor does he readily connect to others emotionally. At the same time, he smiles at those he encounters and likes being with them for limited amounts of time. But he does not need extensive love, he says, which is why he lives alone.
>
> One's first response to this scenario might be to distinguish between the need to be loved and feeling the need . . . This response is no doubt right. But it will not do any good to point it out to him. For he will simply say, "I do not feel that need. Others might feel it, but I do not." It is tempting to accept this reply at face value. But this would be to give up too easily. For there might be things he can do that would cause him to feel the need . . . These ways of getting the emotional hermit to feel the need to be loved may encounter obstacles. It may be his childhood family experiences preventing him from feeling the need. Perhaps his parents were indifferent and unaffectionate toward him. Or perhaps he has frequently been disappointed when investing himself in friendship or love relationships.[13]

It is often the case that atheists and agnostics have had similar stories of disappointment with God. Bart Ehrman is one such agnostic who admits that he lost his faith, not because he felt no desire for God, but because he was disappointed with the amount of evil in the world. In fact,

---

11. Ibid., 119.
12. Ibid., 120.
13. Ibid., 123.

his desire for faith made it very difficult for him to disconnect from it. He explains,

> Eventually, though, I felt compelled to leave Christianity altogether. I did not go easily. On the contrary, I left kicking and screaming, wanting desperately to hold on to the faith I had known since childhood and had come to know intimately from my teenaged years onward. But I had come to a point where I could no longer believe. It's a very long story, but the short version is this: I realized that I could no longer reconcile the claims of faith with the facts of life. In particular, I could no longer explain how there could be a good and all-powerful God actively involved with this world, given the state of things. For many people who inhabit this planet, life is a cesspool of misery and suffering. I came to a point where I simply could not believe that there is a good and kindly disposed Ruler who is in charge of it.[14]

Ehrman's story reminds us of those people who have detached themselves from emotional relationships due to previous relationship disappointments. This does not prove they have no *need* for relationship or to be loved. It only proves that they have psychologically set aside these needs to the point that they might even deny they have ever had them at all. Clearly Ehrman had a desire for God. But his disappointments with the "facts of life" and "suffering" motivated him to push aside this desire. Whatever else might be said about Ehrman's case, the main point here is that natural desires and needs are not necessarily coercive. We can push them aside for various reasons or we may come to a point where we may no longer be aware that we even have them. This is especially true with regard to natural needs that are social or psychological in nature.

These answers can, at least, help one to understand why people can have the desire Lewis spoke of and still deny that they have ever experienced it. Karl Rahner expresses this profoundly, saying, "A person can also hide from himself his transcendental orientation towards the absolute mystery which we call God. As scripture says (Rom. 1:18), he can in this way suppress the most real truth about himself."[15]

---

14. Ehrman, *God's Problem*, 3.
15. Rahner, *Foundations*, 54.

Psyche, the Palace, and Some Other Surprising Truths about Unbelief

We must, however, take some space to emphasize an important point. Perhaps we should not overstate the amount of unbelief that exists in the world. At least in America there is evidence that there are very few consistent atheists. Take for example a relatively recent poll done by The Pew Forum on Religion and Public Life. They polled 36,000 adults and found that 92 percent of Americans believe that there is a God or a "universal spirit."[16] Less than two percent considered themselves "atheists." What was interesting is that even among those who called themselves "atheists," one in five still claimed to believe in some "spirit" or higher power. According to Smith, some of those who said they were atheists, "Later told us they believe in God. This could indicate that some people identify with the term atheist without fully understanding the definition of that term. It could also mean that they identify culturally with atheists, or that they have a negative view of organized religion even though they themselves believe in God."[17]

Half of those who identified themselves as "agnostic" believed in a higher power. While this study only included Americans, there is no reason to suppose that the findings are not consistent with what we see throughout the world in general.[18] Thus, even though there are exceptions to the rule, humans are naturally spiritually inclined. But, someone may still insist, if this is the case, why should unbelief exist in the world *at all*? And if God really wants us to believe in him, why does he not make his presence more visible to us? Taliaferro offers a similar probing question: "If there is a God why isn't God experienced more consistently or pervasively?"[19] Taliaferro then goes on to offer this response: "Perhaps God is experienced more, but we are not as readily aware of this as we might be."[20]

---

16. Smith, "Survey."
17. Ibid.
18. Kai-Man Kwan states, for example, that "Religious believers are still the overwhelming majority of the world's population (84 percent), while nonreligious people are the minority (16 percent)." In Kwan, "Argument," 514.
19. Taliaferro, "Defense," 104.
20. Ibid.

Why Do Some People Never Experience What C. S. Lewis Calls "Joy"?

To reinforce Taliaferro's point, there is an important and helpful illustration in Orual's experience with the invisible palace in C. S. Lewis's fictional work *Till We Have Faces*. After Orual's sister Psyche was sacrificed to the god (which turns out to be marriage and not death) she goes to live in a palace on the Grey Mountain. Not knowing if Psyche was dead or alive, Orual remained heartbroken and angry because, in either case, the god had taken away her sister. Thus, she journeyed toward the mountain where her sister had been "sacrificed." If Psyche was found alive, Orual was determined to get her back from what she consciously believed was a horrible god. When she arrived, to her amazement, she found Psyche alive. Psyche was not just alive, she was more fully happy than ever before. Angered even further by a feeling of betrayal, Orual begged her sister to come back home with her. But Psyche insisted that she already had a home with the god in the palace.

When Psyche went to show Orual the palace, it was not there; or at least it was not visible to Orual.[21] More determined, Orual wanted to break Psyche of her "delusion" that there was any palace or god, and sought all the harder to bring her back home: "'Have done with it, Psyche,' I said sharply. 'Where is this god? Where the palace is? Nowhere—in your fancy.'"[22]

Later, after Psyche and Orual departed, Orual went back with her friend Bardia. When they were to spend the night not far from where she and Psyche spoke, Orual looked toward the direction of the palace. And there she suddenly got a quick glimpse of what she had thought was never there.

> For when I lifted up my head and looked once more into the mist across the water, I saw that which brought my heart into my throat. There stood the palace, grey—as all things were grey in that hour and place—but solid and motionless, wall within wall, pillar and arch and architrave, acres of it, a labyrinthine of beauty.[23]

Just when she was gathering her thoughts about how she should apologize to Psyche and to the god, she also maintained in her senses a ray of doubt that what she was seeing could be real. Then as she stood on her feet "the whole thing vanished."

21. Lewis, *Faces*, 119–20.
22. Ibid., 122.
23. Ibid., 132.

The Apologetics of Joy

> There was a tiny space of time in which I thought I could see how some swirling of the mist had looked, for the moment, like towers and walls. But very soon, no likeness at all. I was staring simply into a fog, and my eyes smarting with it.[24]

What she says next gets to the point to be made here. As she pondered what she had seen, she renewed her sense of disbelief, saying,

> And now, you who read, give judgment. That moment when I either saw or thought I saw the House—does it tell against the gods or against me? Would they (if they answered) make it a part of their defense? say it was a sign, a hint, beckoning me to answer the riddle one way rather than the other? I'll not grant them that. What is the use of a sign which is itself only another riddle? It might—I'll allow so much—it might have been a true seeing; the cloud over my mortal eyes may have been lifted for a moment. It might not . . . Either way, there's still mockery in it. They set the riddle and then allow a seeming that can't be tested and can only quicken and thicken the tormenting whirlpool of your guess-work. If they had an honest intention to guide us, why is their guidance not plain?[25]

This scene cuts to the heart of Beversluis's objection. Why do we not all see the "palace"? And why, if it's there, do we only get hints of it? If it is a natural and innate desire in us all, why can there still be disbelief? And why does God not make his "guidance" clearer?

But as we later learn in the story, the problem was not the invisibility of the palace, but rather Orual's eyes. Without giving any more details away, one of the many points of the story is that people, not God, are the cause for not hearing the echoes of heaven. The fallen condition of mankind is the reason he does not see the divine fingerprints imprinted on every part of the creation around him. According to Lewis, it is our eyes and not God's hands that hide us from the truth. Humanity's fallen condition serves as a reason for not understanding the meaning of the "invisible" palace. For it is not the palace that is invisible, it is man's addiction to the physical world that makes it invisible *to him*. It can either be the lack of imagination, humility, or perception that prohibits him from seeing "the palace" he so desires. But more than anything else, it is sin that keeps him from being able to see. Consequently, according to the moral of the story, man does not see because he is not yet ready to see.

24. Ibid.
25. Ibid., 133–34.

Why Do Some People Never Experience What C. S. Lewis Calls "Joy"?

There is nothing about the palace that makes it so invisible. It is man's own "face" that keeps him veiled to the truth of the palace. Thus man will never see the object of the soul's greatest longing until he has the right kind of humble "face" to see it (thus the book's name, *Till We Have Faces*).

At the end of the book, Orual learns this lesson,

> I know now, Lord, why you utter no answer. You are yourself the answer. Before your face questions die away. What other answer would suffice? Only words, words; to be lead out to battle against other words . . .[26]

God seems hidden to many of humanity's questions because any answer now would simply generate more questions, like a parent trying to explain deep things to a child who is not yet ready to understand what he longs to know. This is the child's *Sehnsucht* (i.e., longing without full satisfaction). This is the adult's too. There is tendency in human nature to long for God, but there is the tendency to push him away as well. God is the source of the former, while we are the source of the latter. It is as Pascal said, "If there were no obscurity man would not feel his corruption: if there were no light man could not hope for a cure. Thus it is not only right but useful for us that god should be partly concealed and partly revealed, since it is equally dangerous for man to know God without knowing his own wretchedness as to know his wretchedness without knowing God."[27]

Thus this sense of desire for the divine can be universally possessed without its object being universally identified or understood.

Before leaving the discussion concerning Orual and Psyche, one more observation should be made. While Orual struggled to see the palace because of her own blindness, it was Psyche's innocence that let her see it even in the imagination of her childhood. Before going up to the Mountain to be sacrificed to the god she expressed her faith and divine desire (*Sehnsucht*) to her sister, saying,

> "Orual," she said, her eyes shining, "I am going, you see, to the Mountain. You remember how we used to look and long? And the stories of my gold and amber house, up there in the sky, where we thought we should never really go? The King of all was going to build it for me. If only you could believe it, Sister! No, listen. Do not let grief shut up your ears and harden thy heart . . . The

---

26. Ibid., 308.
27. Kreeft, *Christianity*, 249.

The Apologetics of Joy

> sweetest thing in all my life has been the longing—to reach the Mountain, to find the place where all the beauty came from . . . Do you think it meant nothing, all the longing? The longing for home? For indeed it now feels not like going, but like going back. All my life the god of the Mountain has been wooing me. Oh, look up once at least before the end and wish me joy. I am going to my lover. Do you not see now?"[28]

Psyche's answer here to Orual seems to be a good answer to Beversluis's objection. Some people will have eyes to see and ears to hear and some people will not. As Williams observes, "We resist faith in God because we see that we would have to give up the self-concern that so occupies our energy and the autonomy that we prize. We do not want to let go of the dear self, so we are blinded to the value of faith in God."[29]

But like Orual at the end of the story, it was never too late for her to open her eyes up again to see what she once saw on the Mountain as a child. Like Psyche, she was once again in tune with the ever-present transcendent desires of her heart "wooing" her back home.

Williams concludes his own book with this vivid point, "We humans find ourselves with certain deep and abiding needs. We don't know why we have them. Yet they are present in us, calling for a response. We need to love, so we love. We need meaning, so we do meaningful things. We need to kneel, so we kneel."[30]

---

28. Lewis, *Faces*, 75–76.
29. Williams, *Reasons*, 181.
30. Ibid., 183.

PART 3

Haunted by Desire

Introduction

THUS FAR THE DISCUSSION of the Argument from Desire has been presented primarily from the works of C. S. Lewis. To help understand his thinking, there was the need to define what Lewis meant by the critical term Joy (or *Sehnsucht*), which is so illuminating to his argument. To further understand Lewis, a comparison was made of his ideas to those found in great thinkers such as Rudolf Otto, Alvin Plantinga, and Karl Rahner. The discussion then turned to how his argument can be laid out formally through inductive and deductive approaches. In part 2 we discussed many of the objections to Lewis's argument that John Beversluis presented in his critical book on Lewis's thought and philosophy.

Here in part 3, we will further elaborate on the nature and role of the second premise of the argument. It is agreed by many that the second premise is the "crucial part of the argument."[1]

Thus, while not neglecting the importance of the first premise (we have dealt with it in previous chapters), we choose to focus here on the second since this is the premise that presents a greater challenge for those who tend to be suspicious of the argument. Additionally, the second premise is also the most subjective of the premises so it will serve to be the most important by way of demonstrating the strength or weakness of the argument. Recall that the second premise states that there is a natural (or innate) desire in humans that nothing on earth can fully satisfy. If we accept the first premise, which says that all natural desires have objects that satisfy them, then the conclusion would follow from this second premise that there must be some object beyond the natural world that serves to satisfy this desire.

The above point therefore begs the question: Is there such a desire that nothing in the natural world can satisfy? In what follows we will offer a discussion that tries to demonstrate that there are natural triggering mechanisms (we will also call them "echoes") in the world that direct man's attention beyond himself to something more. For example, human

---

1. Holyer, "Argument," 70

beings seem to be in a habit of searching for something beyond the physical universe to satisfy a craving for meaning, God or gods, and/or some kind of afterlife. As even atheist writer Matthew Alper states: "Yet with all our knowledge, there still remains that one ever-elusive piece of the puzzle, that one mystery which looms tauntingly over all of the physical sciences, and that is the problem of God. This more than anything else seems to be humankind's ultimate challenge, that one riddle which—should it ever be resolved—might possibly grant us that definitive picture for which we've so painstakingly been searching."[2] Alper goes on to explain that "every human culture has perceived reality as consisting of two distinct substances or realms: the physical and the spiritual,"[3] and then again, "every culture has maintained a belief in some form of spirituality."[4]

In saying all this, Alper seems to be affirming the second premise of the Argument from Desire. Of course, Alper later asserts that God is merely the product of the human brain having been evolved to avoid the fear of death. In part 4 we will deal with this latter point. But for now we simply note that Alper (and many atheists like him) admits that God (or some kind of transcendent reality like God) is a natural human desire that nothing on earth can satisfy. Thus, for atheists like Alper, even though the "painstaking search" for God will always come up empty handed, the natural, innate, and unavoidable "quest would have to go on." In the next few chapters we will take a look at why Alper is right to say that this desire for God is a natural one that cannot find any full satisfaction in this world. But, as stated before, we will also demonstrate that the world offers us many signs that teach us we do not have to end the search empty-handed as Alper suggests. It might be true that we are unable to find full satisfaction for our transcendent desires on earth, but earth may still be giving us clues to keep us looking elsewhere.

2. Alper, *Part*, 2.
3. Ibid., 3.
4. Ibid.

CHAPTER 10

Echoes and Evidences of the Second Premise

As demonstrated above, every culture throughout time has had a tendency to look toward something higher than itself. From aboriginal to modern man, history is filled with worship of transcendental entities. Humans do not always know what it is they are looking for; but they are always looking for, and worshipping, *something*. This, in essence, is what the second premise of the argument states in so many words: there exists an innate desire (*Sehnsucht*) that nothing on earth or in time can fully satisfy.

In *Surprised by Joy* Lewis learned through experience that nothing in his life could satisfy the real desire he craved. However, as is evident in works like his sermon *The Weight of Glory*, Lewis believed that humans live in a world that continuously lures them toward that transcendent Joy. Since it seems that the most important evidence for this second premise comes from a person's own first-person experience, one way to apologetically approach this is to look for hints of transcendence in our experience of the world around (as well as within) us. Lewis believed that while we do not find anything that satisfies this longing in this world, still "we cannot hide it because our experience is constantly suggesting it."[1] In part 3 we seek to discuss a few of the many "experiences that suggest" this transcendence to us. It is written with the same goal as George Steiner when he described his own work as a study that would "contend that the wager on the meaning of meaning, on the potential of insight and response when one human voice addresses another, when we come face to face with the

---

1. Lewis, *Weight*, 30.

text and work of art or music, which is to say when we encounter the other in its condition of freedom, is a wager on transcendence."[2]

Nature's Supernatural Message

Another way of thinking about this is to think of it in what might be called "living echoes" of transcendence.[3] An "echo" is only the reflection or reverberation of the original sound or voice that caused it. It is similar to a sign that points toward something besides itself. Yet an echo is more than a sign. It is a voice or sound of something more real or more foundational than itself. The echo of a voice suggests a subject from which the voice originated. In hearing the echo we do not necessarily see the source of the sound. But the echo suggests the source just the same. When we speak in this chapter of "echoes of transcendence" we are suggesting that the world is filled with sounds that reflect a voice from a source we do not yet see. But before moving on to discuss the specifics of these "echoes" we need to ask what exactly we mean by "transcendence."

Related to the word "transcendence" is the word "sublime." The word sublime refers to something that is "worthy of adoration or reverence." It means "lifted up or set high." In aesthetics, the sublime "is the quality of greatness, or vast magnitude, whether physical, moral, intellectual, metaphysical, aesthetic, or spiritual." It involves that which is "characterized by or eliciting feelings of grandeur, nobility, or awe."[4] Thus, to be sublime is to transcend or hover beyond the normal or the ordinary.

Life is filled with things sublime. When referring to poetry, the ancient writer Longinus says that "the effect of elevated language upon an audience is not persuasion but transport."[5] Thus, "transport" is related to transcendence as well. For Longinus, the idea of transport means that poetry is to do more than just persuade or inform the reader. It is designed to carry the reader away emotionally and intellectually in order to transcend the typical way of thinking about a subject. Poetry does not just give answers. It gives a sense of wonder. But this is not just true of poetry.

2. Steiner, *Presences*, 4.

3. Lewis himself referred to these "pleasures of life" as a "copy or echo" of the "real thing" in *Mere Christianity* (137).

4. *New International Webster's Collegiate Dictionary of the English Language*, 732.

5. Roberts, *Longinus*, 43.

The Argument from Desire assumes that this is also true of all life as well. Life is designed not simply to give us answers but to call us into a sense of wonder. It is by means of our very lives that this "holy mystery"[6] intends to win over our hearts, and not just to inform our intellects.

As Pascal observed, "The heart has reasons that reason knows nothing of."[7] This does not mean that feelings should override intellect. It means that the "heart" actually has *reasons*. There are reasons that resonate in the human heart even when they cannot be communicated through logical demonstration or formal deduction. The complexities of human imagination and understanding are such that they cannot be confined to formal rational processes alone.

What Fairy-Stories, Beauty, and Leisure Can Tell Us About God

As will be discussed in further detail below, one reason we humans love fairy tales so much is that they tell us something about life in ways that are outside of the norm. They make us see things differently. But in a hidden sort of way they also remind us that even the normal world is really not as normal as it first appears. The only reason we do not call gravity a miracle is because we see it at work all the time. If resurrections happened every day, atheists would find a natural reason for them and still reject miracles. Maybe this is why only children have the reputation of enjoying fairy tales. They are not yet used to the world as they find it. In this way, children are touched by the sublime in ways that adults often struggle with. The greatest of poets have been able to retain that child-like quality of seeing the world anew. They still see the extraordinary in what everyone else sees as ordinary. What is mundane to some is still a miracle to others. But it is these who still see the miracle in the ordinary that can best appreciate and create the sublime.

In many ways, the sublime also helps us understand suffering in our world. The evil of pain is not the pain itself. It is that it has invaded our world and has infiltrated into these miracles of life. Suffering feels so wrong because we know that it hinders us from seeing (even for the moment) the good that God has created. But the sublime can take us back to

6. Rahner, *Foundations*, 65–66.
7. Kreeft, *Christianity*, 231.

seeing. It can transport God's children out of the pain and can serve as a signpost that there is a better world outside this one. To say it in biblical terms, the sublime transports us to wonder and glory even while in the despair of Gethsemane.

This is what philosophers and poets like Plato, Longinus, Boethius, Augustine, Auden, and Aquinas were trying to tell us. This transportation of beauty points us toward another world. It is as if the whole world is trying to tell us something and it is the job of poets, philosophers, musicians, and priests alike to remind us in ever so incomplete ways of what that something is.

Like imagination, the Argument from Desire also asserts that an innate hunger for beauty points intentionally toward the divine. Many people today are unaware of the connection. For instance, much of modern culture (especially many in the academic world) seems to have completely removed divine transcendence from the element of beauty. This is seen on nearly every popular beauty magazine where women are valued as objects to be used and lusted after. This is apparent whenever advertisers display humor, entertainment, and art solely to sell a product or to achieve some other utilitarian purpose.

Leisure, play, and love are other human experiences that signal a transcendent reality. These, as will be later demonstrated, have also been sorely misconceived. But while the demoting of imagination, beauty, leisure, and sex is a real problem, the proper perspective and use of them can be interpreted as descending echoes from which perfect imagination, beauty, leisure, and love flow. This is not an affirmation of an abstract world of Platonic forms. Rather it is a call to hear the voice of God in the general revelation of his creation.

In what follows in the next three chapters, some specific elements of the human experience that hint at the divine will be examined. A few of the "signals of transcendence" that Berger speaks of will be discussed. So far we have alluded to these signals in general terms. In Lewis's terms, these chapters will examine certain current experiences of the world that "bear at best only a symbolical relation to what will truly satisfy."[8] Thus, what follows in the next few chapters are not experiences that *satisfy* the Joy Lewis was after. They merely serve to continue to push us in that direction. They serve to inspire us to look upward and to desire more

---

8. Lewis, *Weight*, 29.

Echoes and Evidences of the Second Premise

than what they themselves are able to offer. In other words, this act of "pushing" and "transporting" tells us experientially that the conclusion of the Argument from Desire is true. Namely, there must exist something, outside of time and earth, which satisfies these "echoes" or "signs" of transcendence. The proposition here is that it is perfectly natural and rational to think that there really is a transcendent object (or subject) that these signs point to.

It is important to remember, however, that the discussion that follows does not *prove* that something like God exists. It simply *suggests* it. No one point stands on its own as irresistible evidence for the divine. These echoes serve as kinds of clues that inductively lead us toward a conclusion. As McGrath once noted,

> A clue is something that suggests, but does not prove. Clues have a cumulative significance, pointing to a deeper pattern of meaning that gives each of them their true meaning. One clue on its own might be nothing more than suggestive, a straw in the wind. Yet a cluster of clues begins to disclose a comprehensive pattern. Each clue builds on the others, giving them a collective force that transcends their individual importance.[9]

Yet while there are many such "pointers" or "echoes of transcendence," we only consider three of them here. We select these three (imagination, beauty, and leisure) because these are three major pointers C. S. Lewis suggested in many of his own writings but are probably the least discussed in Christian apologetics in general. Two other major pointers for Lewis were the arguments from morality and reason. But for a detailed discussion of these arguments I refer you to important works found in the bibliography of this book such as "The Moral Argument," from *The Blackwell Companion to Natural Theology*, written by Mark Linville, and *C. S. Lewis's Dangerous Idea: The Argument from Reason*, written by Victor Reppert.

---

9. McGrath, *Mere Apologetics*, 95.

CHAPTER 11

Imagination and the Heart's Deep Need for a Happy Ending

As DISCUSSED ABOVE, LEWIS contends that one of the ways people explain away our natural longing for God is to dismiss it as a childish belief similar to the belief in Santa Claus or the Tooth Fairy. "Of course," says Lewis, "one feels like that when one's young. But by the time you get to my age you've given up chasing the rainbow's end."[1] This, according to Lewis, is the "Way of the Disillusioned 'Sensible Man.'" He is the strictly analytical and scientific type who will only believe what he sees. He agrees with the apostle Thomas, who said, "Unless I see . . . I will not believe" (John 20:25). Thomas would have nothing to do with anything that did not give sufficient empirical evidence. Anything less would be wishful fairy tales that have no grounding in rational thought.

Sigmund Freud is one such thinker who compared the desire for God to a child's wishful thinking as expressed in fairy tales. He states that "When the children were being told a fairy story and were listening to it with rapt attention, he would come up and ask: 'Is that a true story?' When he was told it was not, he would turn away with a look of disdain. We may expect that people will soon behave in the same way towards the fairy tales of religion . . ."[2]

Thus, according to many skeptics, gods and fairies are only for those who have not yet become educated. Richard Dawkins follows this line of thinking when he writes *The God Delusion* and dedicates the book to

---

1. Lewis, *Mere Christianity*, 136.
2. Freud, *Future*, 29.

Douglas Adams, who writes, "Isn't it enough to see that a garden is beautiful without having to believe that there are fairies at the bottom of it too?"[3]

Are "Fairy Tales" Really Just for Children?

One may agree that gardens can be beautiful with or without fairies. But the question becomes whether or not fairies have a place in intelligent conversation at all. A great caution must be made against any modern or scientific ideas that might suggest that the empirical elements of gardens are all we should think about. At the foundation of the above quotes by Dawkins and Freud lies a historically modernist division between the role of the senses and the imagination. Scientism is the view that only things we can see and touch are real. It suggests that gardens are real because we can see them. Fairies are not because we do not see them. The concern here is not so much whether one believes in fairies or not. The concern here is *why* one chooses whether or not to believe them. But are there any good reasons to pay a greater attention to the role that fairies play in the imagination of man?

Lewis offers good reasons why even adults should pay more attention to fairies. When we see the billions of stars at night we cannot help but have a sense of awe. When we see the sun give off light and life, we cannot help but to appreciate its splendor and brightness. That is why "We have peopled air and earth and water with gods and goddesses and nymphs and elves—that, though we cannot, yet these projections can, enjoy in themselves that beauty, grace, and power of which Nature is the image."[4]

This is not to suppose that we should create idols in the skies to worship. But it explains why we are tempted to. And this explains why humans create the stories of myths that they do. One cannot help but think that something else must be "out there" to have created such an imaginative world. Such an inspiration often serves as the motivation for the creation of fairy-stories.

But if believing in fairies is so silly, what makes them such an important historical part of the human experience? What is it about fairy tales that we love so much? Of course most adults today just forget about them.

---

3. Dawkins, *Delusion*, quote from the dedication page.
4. Lewis, *Weight*, 42–43.

The Apologetics of Joy

Fairy tales have been thought to only be for children. This idea has been adopted by our culture since the rise of the scientific revolution. Today, many believe that adults are supposed to know better. For many people, fairy tales are for children and scientific knowledge is for adults. They believe that there are laws that control this world and one should not believe in superstitious nonsense like talking animals and fairy godmothers. But for Lewis the opposite is true. Children are the ones who are closer to the truth. It is adults who have begun to lose their imaginative way. He states his conviction that fairy-stories "are now associated with children" only because they have become "out of fashion" with adults.[5] But Lewis is convinced that "a book worth reading only in childhood is not worth reading even then. The inhibitions which I hoped my stories would overcome in a child's mind may exist in a grown-up's mind too, and perhaps be overcome by the same means."[6]

So what if it is these skeptical adults who are wrong in giving up fairy-stories? What if the child knows something that the skeptic has forgotten? What if secular science has sought to make us believe that fairies are not real when they really, at least in some sense, could be (or at least serve to lead us to a world that is)? Secular scientists would have us only believe what we can see. Some of them try to tell us that the only intelligent thing to do is to believe things that are subject to scientific analysis. The message of scientism is that the mystical stories like Pinocchio and Cinderella must remain in children's books.

But what is it about fairy-stories that draw children to them? And why do adults either love them or (as most often the case) leave them alone? Anthony Esolen has written an important book with these concerns. In fact, he writes with an ironic tone, exploring how culture effectively removes imagination from children. He explains that "Not everyone is a poet, yet children come uneasily near to it in their natural fascination with anything at all."[7] The way to remove imagination from children is to stifle this informing curiosity. By doing this, one can be more effective at keeping quite this longing for transcendence. Sadly, according to Esolen, much of American public education and culture is doing just this.

---

5. Lewis, *On Stories*, 48.
6. Ibid.
7. Esolen, *Ways*, 37.

But such a curiosity comes with the package of every little boy and girl coming into the world. This is not to say that they have a pre-knowledge of stories (as in the case of Plato's pre-recollection of the pre-embodied life of the soul). But it only means that they have pre-disposed faculties that develop to overflow with imagination. As was mentioned above, to infants everything is a miracle. Normal play is considered an adventure (think of peek-a-boo). However, when we get into late adolescence it is no longer "cool" to believe in Barney or Santa Claus anymore. Adolescence is a time when we are encouraged to accept "real life" (however one defines that). And by the time we get to adulthood we have gotten past those "silly stories" and have dug ourselves into the "reality" of the visible world we so commonly experience.

But what if what we believe is "real life" is not the only reality out there? What if fairy tales are loved so much because there is something about them that is natural to believe? Maybe humans come into this world thinking that everything is a miracle because everything really is a kind of miracle. The problem is not what children believe. Maybe the problem is that too many adults have stopped believing. Rudulf Otto states the point beautifully, "As regards fairy-stories, these presuppose the 'natural' impulse to fantasy, narrative, and entertainment, and its products. But the fairy-story proper only comes into being with the element of the 'wonderful', with miracle and miraculous events and consequences, i.e., by means of an infusion of the numinous. And the same holds good in an increased degree of myth."[8]

While we discussed what Otto meant by "numinous" above, we emphasize here that it includes a "feeling of dependence" upon something outside and higher than ourselves. This natural sense comes into this world along with every one of us in such a way that, if science did not "know" any better, it would appear to have been planted there intentionally. Of course, behaviorists deny that we come into this world with anything. Some forms of the view are still lingering which says we come into this world as a "blank slate." The only way humans develop or come to know or believe anything is through the senses. Yet as Mary Midgley so aptly stated,

> How do all the children of eighteen months pass the news along the grapevine that now is the time to join the subculture, to start

8. Otto, *Idea*, 122.

> climbing furniture, toddling out of the house, playing with fire, breaking windows, taking things to pieces, messing with mud, and chasing ducks? For these are perfectly specific things which all healthy children can be depended on to do, not only unconditioned but in the face of all deterrents.[9]

But with whatever else one may come into the world, is it not possible that our natural longing for the divine was put there by something divine? Many secular scholars and scientists think not. Lewis challenged this naturalistic worldview in all of his writings. According to Gregory Bassham, this is one reason Lewis and Tolkien wrote fairy-stories in the first place. In fact, Bassham mentions six important reasons for their doing so. But space will only allow us to mention three of the most pertinent ones for our purposes. First, Lewis wrote fantasy because it "broadens our perspective and enlarges our sense of what is possible."[10] Fantasy can open our eyes to possibilities we would never dream of otherwise. Second, fantasy "can reenchant the ordinary world."[11] As we point out in more detail below, fantasy can make us see ordinary things with a childlike wonder. "By juxtaposing the enchanted with the familiar, the magical with the mundane, fantasy provides us vivid contrasts that help us see the world with fresh eyes."[12] Third, and most applicable to the Argument from Desire, Lewis wrote fantasy because "it can baptize our imaginations."[13] It does this, according to Bassham, by stirring and troubling us "with longing for we know not what, 'a dim sense of something,' beyond our reach . . . In short they can make us feel the beauty of holiness. Such an attraction, Lewis held, can act as a spiritual 'homing signal,' calling us to higher things . . . If pain, as Lewis says, is God's megaphone to rouse a deaf world, the spiritual emotions aroused by good works of literary fantasy are his violin sweetly calling us home."[14]

But maybe this is why the idea of "faith" is waning in our culture (or at least in modern academia). People are failing to see the "homing signals" and deafening themselves from hearing the beauty of the "music" found in fantasy. To borrow from the language of a proverbial phase: modern

9. Midgley, *Beast and Man*, 54.
10 Bassham, "Lewis and Tolkien," 246.
11. Ibid., 247.
12. Ibid., 247–48.
13. Ibid., 254.
14. Ibid.

Imagination and the Heart's Deep Need for a Happy Ending

skeptical scientists fail to see the beauty of the divine forest through the molecular structures of the individual trees. But we need to know that there are alternative views to those that skeptical scientists tell us. Seeing empirically is not always the best, nor the most exhaustive, means of believing. In fact, believing is often the best means of "seeing." Paul, the apostle, explained that people are to be in the business of walking by faith and not by sight (2 Cor 5:7). Jesus also praised those who would believe in him even though they have not seen (John 20:29).

The Miracles of Nature

It might be asserted that this book is encouraging one to have a gullible way of thinking. Nothing that has been suggested so far implies that there does not come a time when we realize that Barney is not a real dinosaur or that there was ever a real puppet named Pinocchio who came to life. What is being suggested here is that humans live in a world where such stories *could* actually happen *if* there was a God who allowed it. What one calls "laws of physics" are not necessarily "laws" at all (at least not in the sense we commonly think of them). They are only events that normally happen by material causes within the *observable* world.

The only reason these "laws" are no longer called miracles is because they are seen at work all the time. If one could turn water into wine every day it would no longer be called a miracle and many would still go around denying that miracles happen. If people rose from the dead all the time no one would call them miracles. They would simply be a part of the "laws" of nature and many naturalists would still think miracles didn't happen. Lewis makes this point succinctly while defining what he understands a miracle to be, saying, "I use the word Miracle to mean an interference with Nature by supernatural power."[15] Thus, for Lewis, a miracle is not something that "breaks" the laws of nature. It is a supernatural "interference" within those laws. For Lewis, the laws of nature are not laws in the sense that they are necessary truths that cannot be interfered with. "By the 'laws of nature' such a man means, I think, the observed course of Nature."[16] The view that the laws of nature are "necessary" truths "seems at first sight to present an insurmountable obstacle to miracle. The break-

15. Lewis, *Miracles*, 5.
16. Ibid., 72.

The Apologetics of Joy

ing of them would, in that case, be a self-contradiction and not even Omnipotence can do what is self-contradictory. Therefore the Laws cannot be broken. And therefore, we shall conclude, no miracle can ever occur?"[17]

But for Lewis such a view is unnecessary. Using the illustration of billiard balls, Lewis explains what he views as a miracle and how it interacts with the laws of nature:

> In the same way, you know what will happen to the two billiard balls—provided nothing interferes. If one ball encounters a roughness in the cloth which the other does not, their motion will not illustrate the law in the way you had expected . . . Or, again, if I snatch up a cue and give one of the balls a little help, you will get a third result: and that third result will equally illustrate the laws of physics, and equally falsify your prediction . . . All interferences leave the law perfectly true. But every prediction of what will happen in a given situation is made under the provisio "other things being equal" or "if there are no interferences" . . . The physicist, as physicist, does not know how likely I am to catch up a cue and "spoil" his experiment with the billiard balls. You had better ask someone who knows *me*. In the same way the physicist, as such, does not know how likely it is that some supernatural power is going to interfere with them.[18]

Thus according to Lewis, "It is, therefore, inaccurate to define a miracle as something that breaks the laws of Nature. It doesn't."[19] Interfering with the laws of nature is not the same thing as breaking them.

Seen in this way, a rose budding in the spring is just as much a miracle as turning water into wine. An infant playing peek-a-boo sees no difference between the appearing and disappearing face and someone turning water into wine. Both actions are interferences of the way things are normally observed by the infant. And he/she would be amazed with both. Try to convince the young child that one is a miracle and one is a "law of nature" and the wonder that is experienced in both events would be just the same to them. As G. K. Chesterton once wrote,

> Just as we all like love tales because there is an instinct of sex, we all like astonishing tales because they touch the nerve of the ancient instinct of astonishment. This is proved by the fact that when we

17. Ibid., 90.
18. Ibid., 90–91.
19. Ibid., 94.

are very young children we do not need fairy tales: we only need tales. Mere life is interesting enough. A child of seven is excited by being told that Tommy opened a door and saw a dragon. But a child of three is excited by being told that Tommy opened the door. Boys like romantic tales; but babies like realistic tales—because they find them romantic.[20]

"But," someone might reply, "the child just doesn't know any better." Their brains have not yet fully developed. Chesterton's contention is that maybe it is the adults who are the ones who often forget the way we are supposed to be looking at life, that it is the adults who are the ones who commonly lose their sense of wonder in the world. The developing logical portions of the brain were never supposed to override our childlike imagination. The logical faculties of the brain are supposed to guide our imagination without destroying it. In this way, "We might think an ordinary flower just that; but to the mind made attentive to the works of nature, the most ordinary things are steeped in their own peculiar ways of being, and are mysterious."[21]

Perhaps this is what Jesus meant when he taught his disciples that they had to become like little children in order to enter the kingdom (Matt 18:3–5; 19:14). Having minds like children enables us to have the faith that empowers us to look at the world in a positively brand-new way. Children humbly believe; adults too often arrogantly doubt. To become like children is appropriate because, as adults, we often grow skeptical of the world. Adults get used to what becomes to them the "laws of nature." But to see it the way God wants us to see it, we must see the world the way we saw it when we first came into it. In this sense everything would be a miracle because everything would be a work of God. The divide between what is a miracle and what is natural would disappear and everything would be seen as divine providence.

But should people really believe in fairies and dragons as adults? Most people already do. Many people believe that certain kinds of fairies are real; they are often called "angels." Many believe that evil dragons really did walk the earth; they call them "extinct dinosaurs." Resurrections do happen all the time; spring season is filled with illustrations of them. Supernatural creation does really happen; it is called "conception" and "birth." Thus, the difference between the adult playing peek-a-boo with

20. Chesterton, Orthodoxy, 49.
21. Esolen, Ways, 37.

the child and Jesus turning water into wine is not *what* is being done. The difference is in *who* is interfering with the normal course of observation. The one who is interfering with the infant's observation of the way things normally are (e.g., seeing a face and then watching it disappear) is a natural being. The one who is turning the water into wine is supernatural. Neither amazements are *violations* of the laws of nature. They both involve someone *interfering* with the way the laws normally operate with respect to the observer. This, as Chesterton pointed out, is also the lure of fairy tales. They give us something that we do not normally see. They amaze us.

What Fairy-Stories Can Tell Us About the World and Humanity

In addition to everything that has already been said about them, there seems always to be *kernels* of truth wrapped in fairy-stories. In fact, we believe there are some things about fairy-stories that engage our true humanity in the guise of creative and fantastic images. But what are they? At least three things come to mind.

First, there is in every fairy-story a *happy ending*. It is commonly recognized that, while there is so much wrong in our world, every part of our being cries out for a happy ending. Fiction writers know that their readers have an inner need for everything to be made right in the end. Thus, this feeling is reflected in the stories they create. Even though there is tragedy in every fairy tale, there is also the happy ending (i.e., what Tolkien calls the "Eucatastrophe" or "good catastrophe"). This does not encourage an extreme escapist view of the world. This does not, as it might sound, defend any mindset that seeks to hide from this world in order to wait it out till the better end. The point of the fairy-story is always one of engagement that calls the characters of the story to participate in bringing about that happy ending. This is what J. R. R. Tolkien was telling us in his insightful work *On Fairy-Stories* when he said, "The consolation of fairy-stories . . . the joy of the happy ending, the sudden joyous 'turn' (for there is no true end to any fairy-tale): this joy . . . is not 'escapist,' not 'fugitive.' In its fairy-tale—or otherworld—setting, it is a sudden and miraculous grace: never to be counted on to recur."[22]

---

22. Tolkien, *Tolkien*, 86.

Second, there is in every fairy-story the theme of a *hero/rescuer*. We all want to know that we are not alone in our tragedies. If Otto, Lewis, and Tolkien are right then there is something in all of us that cries out for help and that knows there is someone listening (recall Otto's "numinous"). This is why it seems that there needs to be (and always is) a hero in every fairy-story.

Third, there is in every fairy-story a theme of *justice*. If we have ever noticed, there is a villain in every fairy-story that either repents or is punished in the end. Both acts reflect a sort of justice that is natural to human desire. Justice is something we all look for in our world. Again, if Lewis and Tolkien are right, this reflects something real in life. As heroes reflect the role of the divine, perhaps villains reflect the satanic themes that run through religious narratives. If justice is, in any sense, a proof of holy transcendence, then the violation of justice must be proof of another side

With these three themes in mind, it may be argued that the Bible contains the greatest story that was ever written, which contains all these elements. God is our hero who saves us (prayer is mankind crying out to our hero). Jesus comes to our rescue (seen in the incarnation and the cross). He will also come one day to judge the world and bring about true justice and the "happy ending" to humanity. These elements are a major reason why many people convert to Christianity. The Gospel appeals to the innermost desires of the human heart. It solves the soul's greatest problems, fills the spirit's most urgent needs, and answers the mind's greatest questions.

There is a sense in which the phrase "In the beginning God created . . ." sounds very close to "Once upon a time . . ." or, better yet, "Once before time . . ." And there is a real sense in which the Bible says that humans can live "happily ever after" in the New Heavens and New Earth. But in comparing the Bible with fairy-stories, I am not, of course, saying that the Bible is exactly like these other stories created by the imaginations of men. My point is that maybe there is more in the fairy tales we read than just the elements of "make-believe."

The story of the Bible reads something like this: "Once upon a time" God created a beautiful world. But a wicked enemy came into that world and tried to take over. But the Creator promised that one day he would come and set everything right. And when that day arrives—when God rules the world by crushing the enemy, man will live "happily ever after."

The Apologetics of Joy

Again, Tolkien concludes *On Fairy-Stories* by saying that the joy that fairy-stories bring

> Looks forward (or backward: the direction in this regard is unimportant) to the Great Eucatastrophe. The Christian joy, the Gloria, is of the same kind; but it is preeminently (infinitely, if our capacity were not finite) high and joyous. But this story is supreme, and it is true. Art has been verified. God is the Lord, of angels, and of men—and of elves. Legend and History have met and fused.[23]

This "Christian joy" is exactly what C. S. Lewis was also getting at in all of his fiction. It is not that the fairy-stories themselves are true. It is as if these fairy-stories are shadows of the true. It is as if these stories are created from minds that are somehow connected to the real transcendent story, hidden away in the human heart, that presses outward in the form of desire (see appendix for more on this point). The human heart may very well be a fallen one. But the Christian story tells of this "good-catastrophe" where the human soul will be redeemed. Both Tolkien and Lewis teach us that every happy ending that has ever been written comes from this longing for redemption. As Tolkien again continues,

> But in God's kingdom the presence of the greatest does not depress the small. Redeemed Man is still man. Story, fantasy, still go on, and should go on. The Evangelium has not abrogated legends, it has hallowed them, especially the 'happy ending' . . . The Christian . . . may now perceive that all his bents and faculties have a purpose, which can now be redeemed . . . All tales may come true; and yet, at the last, redeemed, they may be as like and as unlike the forms that we give them as Man, finally redeemed, will be like and unlike the fallen that we know.[24]

Imagination is one of the strongest hints that the desire for divine worship points toward a real divine being. It is this "primitive wonder that is the source of fairy tales and myths and also of the instinct to worship. We invent preternatural or supernatural objects to incarnate it—elves and wizards and fairies, gods and goddesses—but none of them is it . . . We are possessed by its magic but we do not possess it."[25]

---

23. Ibid., 89.
24. Ibid., 89–90.
25. Kreeft, *Heaven*, 98.

Imagination and the Heart's Deep Need for a Happy Ending

But Lewis tells us that human imagination, while only producing hints of the divine, can be the very tool that points us in the direction of the real thing. In fact, "All the things that have deeply possessed your soul have been but hints of it—tantalizing glimpses, promises never quite fulfilled, echoes that did not die away but swelled into the sound itself—you would know it. Beyond all possibility of doubt you would say, 'Here at last is the thing I was made for.'"[26]

Such a universal and natural sense of imagination, according to writers such as Lewis, Chesterton, and Tolkien, is strong evidence for a transcendent world beyond our own. Again, in the words of Lewis, "I think that all things, in their way, reflect heavenly truth, the imagination not least."[27] Thus the similarities between the Gospel and fairy-stories do not prove the Gospel to be mere make-believe. In fact, according to Lewis, the similarities are *exactly* as one would expect if the Gospel story were found to be true after all.

26. Lewis, *Problem*, 131.
27. Lewis, *Surprised*, 167.

CHAPTER 12

In the Defense of Beauty

IT HAS BEEN ARGUED thus far that there are hints (or echoes) of the divine in the desires of life as expressed in the imagination. This is no less true of the subject of beauty. Yet beauty is a unique reality that comes into human experience. Though they are intimately related, beauty is functionally different than either truth or goodness. As Peter Kreeft affirms, "Though beauty is derived from truth and goodness, it has the greatest power over our souls."[1] While truth connects to our intellect and goodness to our will, beauty touches our emotions in ways that the others cannot. God has made all three: the intellect to have the ability to know; the will to have the ability to define ourselves morally; and beauty to experience the aesthetic power of the world around us. But while we humans enjoy beauty every day, we rarely stop to think very long about the implications it has on our lives as a whole.

The good news is that beauty has been on the rise as an academic discipline.[2] Of course, as stated above, appreciating beauty is nothing new. Music, art, romance, and the sciences have been admiring beauty since the beginning of humanity's ability to experience them. But beauty *qua* beauty has not always shared a well-represented place in modern academic history. It has either fallen prey to the "old-fashioned skeptical scientific materialist of the modern" era or has been distorted by the

---

1. Kreeft, "Philosophy," 25.
2. Roger Lundin has argued that "under the pressure of political events and social change, beauty was significantly eclipsed as a subject of academic interest in the last decades of the twentieth century, but in the past decade that interest has begun to rise once again. Works such as Elaine Scarry's *On Beauty and Being Just* . . . and Denis Donoghue's *Speaking of Beauty* . . . are representative of a vibrant, renewed emphasis upon the centrality of beauty in literary and cultural studies." In Lundin, *Believing Again,* 211–12n.

"newfangled postmodernist subjectivist relativist."³ Kreeft goes on to say, "The old kind of skeptic forbids us to claim that any idea is true or good or beautiful; the new kind forbids us to claim that any idea is false or evil or ugly."⁴ For where there is no such thing as objective truth, there can be no such thing as objective beauty. But true beauty, if identified as the artwork of God, can allow us to view it in its most grand purpose—to glorify its Artist and to make us wonder at his craftsmanship.

That "Other" Beauty

As noted by Lundin, Elaine Scarry is one such scholar who has brought objective beauty back to the academic stage. In her work *On Beauty and Being Just*, she allows for beauty to be a guide that can lead us in the direction of truth and even something divine.

> Something beautiful fills the mind yet invites the search for something beyond itself, something larger . . . One can see why beauty—by Homer, by Plato, by Aquinas, by Dante . . . has been perceived to be bound up with the immortal, for it prompts a search for a precedent, which in turn prompts a search for a still earlier precedent, and the mind keeps tripping backward until it at last reaches something that has no precedent, which may very well be the immortal.⁵

According to Scarry, the beautiful person or thing can "incite" in us the "longing for truth" and the divine since "What is beautiful is in league with what is true because truth abides in the immortal sphere."⁶ But again as Lewis suggested, "These things—beauty, the memory of our own past—are good images of what we really desire; but if they are mistaken for the thing itself, they turn into dumb idols."⁷

This was exactly Plato's point in the *Symposium*. Beauty on earth is something, according to Socrates, that is being experienced in "due order and succession," pointing to "a nature which in the first place is

---

3. Kreeft, "Philosophy," 27.
4. Ibid.
5. Scarry, *On Beauty and Being Just*, 29–30.
6. Ibid., 30–31.
7. Lewis, *Weight*, 30–31.

everlasting, not growing and decaying, or waxing and waning."[8] Earthly beauties are used as "steps" to reach that "other beauty"; a "beauty which if you once beheld, you would see not to be after the measure of gold, and garments, and fair boys and youths, whose presence now entrances you."[9] This very beauty that "entrances" us is what Lewis spoke of in *The Weight of Glory*: "We do not merely want to see beauty . . . We want something else which can hardly be put into words—to be united with the beauty we see, to pass into it, to receive it into ourselves, to bathe in it, to become part of it."[10]

This "entrancing" beauty is what motivates us to practice love and justice. But beauty seen as an end only to itself can become an idol. These idols come in the forms of greed, pornography, adultery, envy, and covetousness. It comes because we think that earthly beauty is enough to satisfy us. But this point is what is at the heart of *Sehnsucht*. Joy (seen as transcendent desire) will never be satisfied by anything on earth no matter how hard one tries. Forms of greed, pornography, adultery, envy, and covetousness are excessive and/or misguided attempts at satisfying *Sehnsucht*. To a lesser or greater degree, all humans will seek to satisfy *Sehnsucht* in unhealthy ways as long as they seek it *solely* in the things of this world. In the words of the writer of Ecclesiastes, everything will feel like "vanity" if satisfaction is only looked for "under the sun."

Beauty in Balance: Plato and Aristotle Working Together

Of course, as in everything humanity does, there is a potential danger in speaking of "earthly" and "transcendent" beauty as if they were always two separate things. Heaven and earth do not possess two different kinds of beauties but rather two manifestations of one divine beauty. The claims that the beauty of creation points to the beauty of the Creator and another world need not negate or diminish the importance of the beauty in this created world. Plato had many wonderful things to say about beauty, but some of what he said assumes a view of the world that is not consistent with the Christian worldview. Plato held that this world was merely made up of copies (or shadows) of the perfect world of ideas (i.e., true forms).

8. Plato, "Symposium," 167.
9. Ibid.
10. Lewis, *Weight*, 42.

He implies a dichotomy and dualism that is unhealthy for creatures that were called by God to care for his beautiful world (see Gen 1:26–28). This world is a "very good" world whose beauty should be appreciated and delighted in (Gen 1:28, 31). While pornography is idolatry, marital sex is still divine. And while beauty is appreciated in the eye of the beholder, it exists outside of the eye as well. Beauty is in the eye of the beholder only if the beholder is divine. For the ancients, God was the definition of beauty. Things are beautiful because they reflect something of his power, love, and nature. This is one reason the apostle Paul was so angry about idolatry in Romans 1. He claimed in verse 20 that the creation puts the spotlight on divine wisdom, not the other way around. Man is to be both content, and even inspired, by the material things of the world, but not controlled and immersed in them. It was Jesus who taught us that "man does not live on bread alone" (Matt 4:4). Manna came down from heaven, it did not define it.

Seeing this imbalanced view of beauty, a pupil of Plato's sought to bring his dualistic world together into one. Aristotle believed that there was no realm of forms out there in some abstract land of ideas. He believed that the forms of the beauty of things were found in the things themselves. Matter and form were no longer in two separate worlds. However, the potential danger in over-emphasizing Aristotle's ideas is that one might forget about earth's "signals of transcendence" that are here to point humanity to the truth that there is indeed a relational separation of heaven and earth through sin. We need to hear Plato's vision of transcendent beauty. But we need to do so while maintaining the divinely created beauty we find on earth. It is not a separation of a world of forms from a world of matter that defines reality. It is the separation of humanity from the Garden of Eden that now defines it. While we now have "signals of transcendence," Adam and Eve had transcendence staring them in the face.

C. S. Lewis believed this separation was caused by a fallen world (i.e., sin) not a separation defined by an inferior existence of physical things to abstract ideals. If Aristotle is read exclusively (perhaps erroneously) one may look down too much and see only the beauty of plants and trees and beasts. But if Plato is read exclusively (perhaps erroneously) one might be tempted to look up too much and think of the forms of invisible souls and abstract worlds. After reading Aristotle and Plato, we need to also turn to

Aquinas and Lewis who help us to see that everything really is beautiful but yet can still point us to a much greater transcendent beauty.

Beauty as Seen in the Middle-Ages: Teacher of the Divine

This last sentence reminds us of another area of history that needs to be discussed in light of the subject of beauty. Following the ancient world of Plato and Aristotle, the association of beauty to the divine was also an important feature of the medieval period. Artists and philosophers during the Middle Ages had constantly connected the beauty of colors and objects to a transcendent source. Not that the things themselves were worshipped, but that, for them, the beauty of life pointed to God in its created purpose. The arts intentionally pointed to the Artist. Lewis makes this clear when he compares how medieval thinkers looked at the universe and how modern science has looked at it. "The really important difference is that the medieval universe, while unimaginably large, was also unambiguously finite."[11] While the functions and movements of the universe are more understood today, a case can be made that the wonder of it was better understood in the Middle Ages. With the finitude of the universe understood, and with mankind seen as the center of it all, God was lifted to the role of infinite Creator. While modern science has sought to take apart the universe in order to understand it, the ancients kept it in one piece so as to feel its divine wonder. "The space of modern astronomy may arouse terror, or bewilderment or vague reverie; the spheres of the old present us with an object in which the mind can rest, overwhelming in its greatness but satisfying in its harmony."[12]

But as humanity's knowledge of the universe has increased, so has its confidence in its own abilities and potential. But, according to the common worldview in the Middle Ages, the downfall of this thinking was the fact that the universe was not made to boost humanity's ego. It was made to show how little humans are and how big God is in comparison to them. Dante's *Divine Comedy*, among other things, has taught us this.

The Modern (and often skeptical) view of the world has made us see the universe as a large expanding accident, growing along with humanity's knowledge that now tells us we evolved only, and only happen, to

11. Lewis, *Image*, 99.
12. Ibid.

be in it. Along with the earth, man has lost his meaningful place at the center of the universe. Of course, there is nothing wrong with opening the human mind to the natural laws of our world. But this should never have allowed us to lose sight of its unified beauty. One could take apart a flower to understand its molecular structure, but in so doing he has lost the flower. In his learning *about* the flower he is tempted to lose sight of its unified beauty. Thus, the medieval thinkers did not just want to know about the parts of the world. They wanted the world itself.

Consequently, understanding the motions of the universe has been both a blessing and a curse. Scientists have found out that the sun does not revolve around the earth. Yet somehow many have forgotten that the world was made in such a way that humans were supposed to feel like it did. Scientists now understand that there is no such thing as an "up" and "down" in space. But should this cause humanity to forget that the world was made to make us feel as though there is? Most of the medieval thinkers knew that the world was not just here for us to break it down and understand it. They believed it was here for us to experience it. In this way, they also believed it was here to glorify its Creator. As one writer put it, "To be sure, they tended to look upon nature as a reflection of the transcendent world."[13]

Thinking Beyond the Stars

This is exactly what is being suggested here. The universe, in all its beauty, is here to tell us something more than how the black hole forms or what happens when galaxies collide. From our phenomenological viewpoint the earth makes us look "upward" to the stars. Consequently, their beauty and wonder makes us feel as though something lies beyond them. The enlightenment thinkers taught us that the world was unimaginably big. But it was the medieval thinkers who taught us that the world was a witness to something infinitely bigger. The stars are not just exploding in and out of existence. They are message bearers telling us that something more is out there beyond them.

But the beauty of the universe is not the only thing bearing witness to transcendence. Art has something to say as well. Yet during the rise of the modern period, many in the West began to lose confidence in the arts as a

13. Eco, *Art and Beauty*, 4.

witness to transcendence. In the eighteenth-century, "prompted by modern cosmology and historical consciousness," art "became further and further separated from reason, and thereby too from the natural world that was now taken to be silent, beauty became an alternative faith."[14] According to Francis Schaffer, "Modern pessimism and modern fragmentation have spread in three different ways to people of our own culture and to people across the world . . . *Culturally*, it spread in the various disciplines from philosophy to art, to music, to general culture . . . and to theology."[15] Thus, beauty and art no longer existed to teach us anything about the world. They only served to make us feel good and give us a sense of pleasure in an otherwise mundane and empty life. Thus the Enlightenment not only ended up separating fact from value and science from religion, it also separated aesthetics from truth, and beauty from objective reality.

But, getting back to the later medieval period, this is originally why Aquinas sought to adapt Aristotle's new appreciation for the beauty of this world into the Christian context. He saw what was on the cultural horizon. And he thought that while the philosopher was limited in what he could know about God, nature could still reveal much of God's wisdom. After all, beauty sprung from God's very creative act. But, unlike Aristotle, Aquinas believed it was no longer just any Unmoved Mover pushing the world along in an infinite chain of causation. God was personal and his love filled the world he created. Thus he created mankind with a nature that would crave transcendence. This is why Aquinas affirmed, "For there resides in every man a natural desire to know the cause of any effect which he sees; and thence arises wonder in man."[16]

Consequently, Aquinas defended his own Argument from Desire by continuing, "But if the intellect of the rational creature could not reach so far as to the first cause of things, the natural desire would remain void."[17] In this way, Lewis and Aquinas were presenting very similar arguments. For Aquinas, this "natural desire" to know the cause of all things led him to wonder. Yet without divine revelation the natural mind remains "void" of concrete answers. Yet the natural desire is still there. For Lewis, this natural desire was for "something more," which led him to "wonder" also.

14. Treier et al., *Beauty*, 14.
15. Schaeffer, *How*, 182.
16. Aquinas, *Summa*, 113.
17. Ibid.

And for both Aquinas and Lewis, this sense of "wonder" gave both a sense of joy and frustration at the same time. Natural theology and philosophy can only take us so far in our search for Joy. But it can (and does) serve to move us closer to the divine (i.e., the "first cause" of all things).

Thus while Aquinas did not think that belief in God was properly basic (i.e., a first principle that needed no demonstrative evidence) he did believe that it could be very quickly ascertained by the combination of the nature and wonders of the world and the *sensus divinitatis* that dwells in us. Because of the beauties of the world, we can quickly begin to long for the divine presence. Lewis agreed, saying, "Nature is only the image, the symbol; but it is the symbol Scripture invites us to use. We are summoned to pass in through Nature, beyond her, into that splendor which she fitfully reflects."[18]

The Rise of the Enlightenment and the Fall of Objective Beauty

But, as stated briefly above, there were new challenges to beauty and transcendence with the rise of the Enlightenment. Skepticism made many suspicious of the external world. W. H. Auden wrote a critical essay identifying the dangers of that period to aesthetics and beauty. In "The Poet and the City" he specifically identified four areas during the eighteenth century that went wrong. In his second point he mentions two leading thinkers who influenced the dramatic change from what had been seen in the Middle Ages. The two individuals were Luther and Descartes.

Luther unwittingly created a movement that saw the external act as something disconnected to internalized faith. Acts of obedience were not a part of internal conversion. This contributed to what Auden saw as "the loss of belief in the significance and reality of sensory phenomena."[19] While Luther himself never intended this, the assumed implications his followers saw in his teaching made the dichotomy inevitable.

An even greater threat to sensual beauty was found in Descartes, who is known as the father of modern philosophy. Descartes placed a greater wedge between the external world of the senses and the internal world of mind. His further distinctions between what John Locke would

18. Lewis, *Weight*, 44.
19. Auden, *Dryer's Hand*, 78.

later classify as "primary qualities" and "secondary qualities" led to a deep mistrust of the external world. Primary qualities are properties an object has that are independent of any observer. They are the properties of things within themselves. If a ball is round, it is round no matter if someone is observing it or not. However, secondary qualities are properties that are dependent on the observer. If the ball is hot, the existence of the sensation of heat is dependent upon the person feeling it. Not everyone will experience the sensation in the exact same way. Of course, this distinction between primary and secondary qualities does not itself create a mistrust of the external world. Nevertheless, Descartes believed that humans could not trust their senses (i.e., secondary qualities) as they relate to the outside world (i.e., the primary qualities) because they are so often deceived by their senses.[20]

This mistrust eventually continued to increase, to the full-blown skepticism of David Hume. But beginning with Descartes, the question now came up as to whether we could ever really trust our senses at all. Was the external world merely a trick of some evil demon? According to Cartesian skepticism the only certainty we possess is the existence of our internal self. Everything else is under suspicion. Of course, Descartes climbed out of this skepticism only by what he perceived was an *a priori* deduction toward a benevolent God. But without this subjective (internal) confidence for Descartes, nothing could be known for certain about the sensual world. This newfound dualistic emphasis created profound implications for man's view of the world and the nature of the beauty it possessed.

According to Auden, the implications and influences of Luther and Descartes were not only profound, but also widespread. In a very short time they taught people to doubt their senses. But if one removes the senses from the assurance of reality anything and everything goes. Nothing out there in the world could be known as beautiful because it was untrustworthy. The poet could only trust his "subjective sensations and feelings," which means that poetry and art came to have no objective meaning at all. But if the external world had no trustworthy meaning, then it was no longer able to tell us anything about transcendence or the divine.

For Luther's followers, baptism was not a sign that connected believers to salvation because, as a symbol, it was completely severed from the "real" thing. Thus all symbols were seen with either suspicion or as threats

---

20. Descartes, *Meditation*, 92–96.

In the Defense of Beauty

to genuine spirituality. As Lundin points out concerning this period, "the separation of aesthetic and rationality—of art and reason—soon became commonplace."[21] But if art is removed from reason, then art has no place in intellectual dialogue. Art and imagination were left to the entertainers, but reason was left to the scientists, and only the scientists were qualified to do the serious research. We do not have to guess which side of that room all forms of fairy-stories and religions fell. As Auden again concludes, "Modern science has destroyed our faith in the naïve observation of our senses: we cannot, it tells us, ever know what the physical universe is really like; we can only hold whatever subjective notion is appropriate to the particular human purpose we have in view."[22]

The Implications of the Secular Age

Thus began the disenchantment of the world. The world became a predictable place where everything operated in Newtonian mechanical laws of nature. The world was no longer an organism, it was a machine. Thus, the danger of science has become to a large extent its removal of teleology and beauty from the study of nature. Whereas the pre-scientific world understood nature to be full of meaning and desire, the scientific revolution demystified nature, transforming it into a spiritless system of cogs and electricity.

Seeing the world this way made the arts something that stood on their own. Not just in the sense that art was created for art's sake, but that art was created by artists who alone give meaning and value to it. In other words, art was exalted as humanity's masterpiece and theirs alone. Beauty began to have no objective meaning. It was all strictly "in the eyes of the beholder." Postmodernism began to arise from the flowering of this subjective mindset. Beauty is, thus, always subject to the context and opinion of the individual situation or person. But, according to Lewis, this is exactly what happens once humanity removes beauty, truth, and value from God. We become the gods who make beauty rather than discover it. Lewis brings this out in his *Letters to Malcolm*: "What makes some theological works like sawdust to me is the way the authors can go on discussing how far certain positions are adjustable to contemporary

21. Lundin, "Beauty," 189.
22. Auden, *Dryer's Hand*, 78.

thought, or beneficial in relation to social problems, or 'have a future' before them, but never squarely ask what grounds we have for supposing them to be true accounts of any objective reality. As if we were trying to make rather than learn. Have we no Other to reckon with?"[23]

The problem comes when human beings see themselves as self-sufficient and art becomes the symbol of that self-sufficiency. A discussion of the dividing of *liberal* arts and *useful* arts comes into play here.[24] Liberal arts are truly liberal when humans are free to create for no other purposes except for the sake of the true beauty the created thing reflects. Beauty itself should be seen in the very act of creating. As artists and imitators of God we participate in the arranging of this beautiful world. However, *useful* art is valued only for what it can do for humanity. Whatever makes life better is what is now valued as the greatest kind of art today. But seen in this way, art is no less than idols fashioned in order to satisfy humanity's desires and purposes. This is the very thing C. S. Lewis said must not be allowed to happen. For even the very best art this world offers will never fully satisfy the longing (i.e. *Sehnsucht*) that man experiences. Truly, we do have an "Other to reckon with," and it is this beauty alone that defines and objectifies ultimate reality.

Consequently, if we put too much trust in the arts and too much admiration in the creation, it becomes the god itself (see Rom 1:18–25). The beauty of earth must not be allowed to serve as an idol. We must not allow ourselves to think "that earth can be made into heaven."[25] Art and poetry cannot save the world. Art can be as pluralistic as anything else sub-created by humanity. Jacques Barzun warns of this in *The Use and Abuse of Art*:

> How can Art, diverse and diffused as it is, remonstrate with all these miscreants, much less reform them? The artist is not and cannot be the close minister of each individual spirit and nothing short of this relation can be reformative and religious. The artist says quite properly that not he but his work is the carrier of truth. If so, the religious idea of art collapses altogether: having no unity, no eternity, no theology, no myth, no minister, its cult can only fall

---

23. Lewis, *Letters*, 104.
24. Lundin, "Beauty," 189–90.
25. Lewis, *Weight*, 31.

into a worship of the instrument—idolatry . . . a dead stop along the way to the transcendent.[26]

Barzun does not want to be misunderstood to say that art cannot serve a divine purpose. He states, "Do not mistake me and think that I am calling the love of art idolatry." Yet he sees a larger issue happening in the modern world where art no longer serves to glorify God but rather becomes god. Art in a secular age tends to get more adoration than it is worth. The Western world has many idols that come in the form of various arts. Thus, Barzun quotes C. S. Lewis as saying, "You will not get eternal life by just feeling the presence of God in flowers and music." He also quotes Hilaire Belloc as saying, "Faith is not a mood but an act—a matter of the will." He then concludes, "Once more, art is irremediably of this world, not of the next."[27]

Nevertheless, even though art is not itself divine, in its purest form it can point us in that direction. Put goodness "above beauty, and beauty flourishes," and so does the art that reflects it.[28] Thus, in the act of the artist, there is found this flourishing beauty where "there is in the experience of meaningful form, a presumption of presence."[29] That is to say, the beauty in art, when properly perceived, can serve to lure us toward the feeling of divine transcendence. According to Lewis, "beauty" in the broadest sense is the name given to the desire we cannot locate on earth. Thus, beauty serves as a divine messenger telling us of another world that contains a beauty superior to itself. As Lewis explains, "A scientist may reply that since most of the things we call beautiful are inanimate, it is not very surprising that they take no notice of us. That, of course is true. It is not the physical objects that I am speaking of, but that indescribable something of which they become for a moment the messengers."[30]

There is still hope that "the currently defaced visage of beauty will one day lead us back to Christ, and to a restoration of all things."[31]

26. Barzun, *Use and Abuse*, 92.
27. Ibid.
28. Kreeft, "Philosophy," 34.
29. Steiner, *Presences*, 214.
30. Lewis, *Weight*, 40
31. Oakes, "Apologetics," 226.

Chapter 13

Lewis, Leisure, and *Sehnsucht*

As SEEN ABOVE, BEAUTY and imagination are pointers (or hints) that haunt our world and offer evidence of divine transcendence and divine presence. They are two of the many things in life that trigger our sense of longing for the eternal. Yet another pointer we will consider here suggests that even the playful and leisure times of life can be divine hints toward the Joy Lewis and others spoke of.

Leisure as Echoing the Divine Life of Contemplation and Rest

In his book *Leisure: The Basis of Culture*, German philosopher Josef Pieper has given an unusually scholarly treatment to a normally casual subject. Although the book was written in 1952 by a German philosopher, one would get the impression that he was writing for our twenty-first-century American Culture.

According to Pieper, "leisure" is that time when we contemplate the things of life that fuel our souls. It is about spending time with our thoughts or the needs of our own souls. Leisure is what you do when you do not have to do anything else. It is that time when we get away from the obligations of life. It is having a sense of joy and peace that only comes from doing nothing at all, nothing that is, except to think, pray, or play.

We could say that "leisure" is spending time with God and with self. It is our choice to remove ourselves from the deadlines of life and from the duties we have to family and to others.

And leisure is not something that just happens to you. You will always have more duties to fulfill. You will always have something pressing that needs to get done. But leisure is something you must force yourself to have. It is the time when you make everything else wait.

To offer a biblical example: While we are not told a lot about the "leisure" times of Jesus, the Gospels do suggest that it was an important part of his life. Of all people, Jesus was one who always had more he could do. There were always more people to teach and more sick people to heal. Yet Matthew 14:13 says that Jesus "departed to a deserted place by Himself." He apparently did this often. Luke 5:16 says that Jesus "often withdrew into the wilderness and prayed." Again, Mark 1:35 states that Jesus "departed to a solitary place, and there He prayed." In our attempt to be more like Christ we must not forget to learn how to rest, how to slow down. We must learn how to experience leisure.

Everyone needs leisure. God "rested" on the seventh day to teach humans that they need to rest (Gen 2:2–3). But leisure means more than just rest. The Greek word for leisure is *skola*. The Latin equivalent is *skole*. These Greek and Latin words are where we also get our English word "school." But what does school have to do with leisure? Leisure is the time when we do our best learning. It is when we spend time with our thoughts and with what James Schall calls our "mental life."[1] Simply put, leisure is essential for our mental health and well-being.

Without leisure we could never do effectively what Paul tells us to do in his letter to the Philippians. Chapter 4:8 reads, "Finally, brethren, whatever things are true, whatever things are noble, whatever things are just, whatever things are lovely, whatever things are of good report, if there is any virtue and if there is anything praise worthy—meditate on these things." To "meditate" means to think deeply on something, to dwell on it for a sufficient period of time. But to meditate on the things that Paul instructs us to means that we need the quiet time set aside to do so. We need to take the time to read and study. We also need the time to reflect on these "higher things" of life. But too often, when we have the quiet time to think, we instead have the feeling of just being "bored." We always seem to want more to do, even when we complain of not having any time to ourselves.

People only get "bored" because their minds have become so used to being busy. When human minds become so used to the fast pace of life, they forget how to slow down. When one reaches a point in the day when

---

1. Schall, *Life*, 7–42.

things do slow down, the mind is less occupied. Those who are not used to "leisure" do not know how to handle this "down time" and they do not know what to do with it. They feel "bored" or, in extreme cases, "depressed." The longer the mind is chaotic and busy the more the adrenaline rushes in. The longer and more the adrenaline high lasts, the more one feels the hangover effects of boredom when it is gone. Thus, we cannot sit still for long. According to Pieper, "Leisure, it must be clearly understood, is a mental and spiritual attitude. It is not simply the inevitable result of spare time, a holiday, a weekend, or a vacation . . . Leisure implies an attitude of in-activity, of inward calm, of silence; it means not being busy, but letting things happen."[2]

Leisure time is not about being "bored." It is about thinking, contemplation, prayer, play, rest, and study. Consequently, neither is leisure about resting up *just so that* we can get back to work on Monday. This would make work the center and purpose of leisure. But leisure is to be valued on its own. It is not a means to our occupational ends. Leisure is not just a time when we "fuel up" in order to get ready for the next workday. On the contrary, one could well argue that we actually go to work so that we can allow ourselves healthy leisure.

Pieper does a much-needed job getting us to think. That, by itself, is a difficult task in our crazy, work-based culture. But he reminds us that there is more to the divine life than just "duty." There is even more to the divine life than "doing." In fact, at regular times the best thing a person can do for him/herself is to do nothing at all. This concept can be related to Lewis's idea of our longing for God. In *Letters to Malcolm* Lewis explains it this way:

> Surely we must suppose the life of the blessed to be an end in itself, indeed The End: to be utterly spontaneous; to be the complete reconciliation of boundless freedom with order—with the most delicately adjusted, supple, intricate and beautiful order? How can you find any image of this in the "serious" activities either of our natural or of our (present) spiritual life? Either in our precarious and heart-broken affections or in the Way which is always, in some degree, *a via crucis*? No, Malcolm. It is only in our "hours off," only in our moments of permitted festivity, that we find an analogy. Dance and game are frivolous, unimportant, down here; for "down here" is not their natural place. Here, they are a moments

---

2. Pieper, *Leisure*, 46.

rest from the life we were placed here to live. But in this world everything is upside down. That which, if it could be prolonged here, would be truancy, is like that which in a better country is the End of ends, Joy is the serious business of heaven.[3]

According to both Pieper and Lewis, it is in the quiet times that we can often hear God best. And it is often in the playful times that we can experience the seriousness of heaven. But in all these times we are experiencing a trigger that prompts an element of transcendence and get us closer to the experience of Joy (*Sehnsucht*). "The child who plays with toys and knows something greater than toys is threatening to the adult who takes his grown-up toys with ultimate seriousness because he does not know of anything greater."[4]

This is why the most frustrated people in the world are often those who have the most possessions. People who are committed to getting riches thrive in the task toward getting them. They are motivated to fill the longing of their hearts through the empty spaces in their wallets. But once they get to where they always wanted to be they are even more frustrated because it did not give them what they thought it would. Not realizing they were being haunted by something that transcends their bank accounts, they maintain their discontented search in the world because what they have so far gained has not satisfied their constant urge for more. Those who have convinced themselves that they are happy because they possess "things" have not yet realized their callous self-deception. If they could look inside of their own hearts they would still see emptiness. They long for more because they have gained too much.

Yet we must mention here that leisure is anything but being idol. The opposite of a leisurely life is a hollow and empty life. Consequently, leisure may very well be the nearest thing we have to compare to what we are really longing for because it offers, at least, some peace of mind and fullness of spirit that other activities do not offer. This is what Aristotle calls the "contemplative life." As he explains, "Contemplation seems to be the only activity loved for its own sake, for nothing comes from it beyond the contemplating, while from things involving action we gain something for ourselves, to a greater or lesser extent, beyond the action. And happiness

---

3. Lewis, *Letters*, 92–93.
4. Kreeft, *Heaven*, 239

The Apologetics of Joy

seems to be present in leisure, and we make war in order that we may stay at peace."[5]

Thus we work so that we can have leisure and not the other way around. James Schall may have been right to say that what is "useless" is the best thing about us.[6]

Leisure as God's "Playfulness" and Ours

But if both Aristotle and Schall are right, then utilitarian workdays are not leisurely at all. But what would this mean for Creation as recorded in Genesis? Work was certainly in Paradise from the beginning (Gen 2:15). However, I suspect that Adam and Eve would never have called "tilling" the Garden of Eden "work" in the utilitarian sense of the word. Life in the Garden was leisurely, not lazy. It was, in every sense of the word, "playful."

While it may not be a fully complete definition, to be at "play" is, at least, to be doing an unnecessary activity that springs from a sense of joy and not out of mere usefulness. While one can play while doing something useful, it is not entirely the same thing. Of course, developmental psychologists may counter that there are many useful benefits in play. Robert Franken suggests many such benefits. First is the benefit a child gets when it is learning to interact with other children.[7] Another benefit of play is the building of a person's creativity. "Creativity is often viewed as playful activity in which we allow ourselves to reorder or recombine things in new and different ways."[8] In this sense there is usefulness in play. But if you ask the child why they are playing, you will never hear it say, "I am doing this because it will help me develop my prefrontal lobe, and will also encourage healthy interaction with co-workers in the future." Children play because it's "fun." They play because they don't have to. And they play because they experience joy from being with others who are acting in unnecessary ways with them.

This point leads us into another thought. If we define "play" to be an unnecessary activity sprung from a sense of joy, then there is a sense in which God's creation of the world can be understood as God being

---

5. Aristotle, *Nicomachean Ethics*, 192.
6. Schall, *Unseriousness*, 158.
7. Franken, *Motivation*, 336.
8. Ibid., 348.

"at play." For instance, the God of the Bible did not have to create. And, unlike the polytheistic gods of the Greeks, he did not get anything *useful* for himself out of making humanity.

Maybe this is why he calls us to do the same. Having dominion over the earth has little to do with being "in charge." It means we participate in the divine act of creation (i.e., what some have called "sub-creation"). The medieval thinkers understood this better than many of our age. "The medieval conception of art was rooted in, and was more or less the same as, the Classical and intellectualist theory of human 'making'" with the creative action beginning with God.[9] They believed that God first created *ex nihilo*, and humans, in turn, take what God created and sub-create their own inventions. They believed in the divine cycle of God creating nature, then nature inspiring art, with art reflecting back on nature, then nature reflecting back to the wisdom of God. This "reflecting back" can be understood as one of the transcendent echoes producing the *Sehnsucht* in humanity.

So because leisure is an act of contemplative creating, maybe this is a shadowy hint of what the citizens of heaven are up to. At least it is a good indication of what it means to engage in the fullness of human flourishing. Thus, as inspiring as humanity's creative abilities on earth can be, they pale in comparison to that ultimate place of Joy Lewis spoke of.

Narnia and the Very "First Joke"

If you will recall in chapter three we talked about Uncle Andrew's skeptical view of Aslan's ability to create talking beasts in Lewis's Narnia book *The Magician's Nephew*. We pointed out that Uncle Andrew could not accept the fact that a lion was actually talking, let alone creating a world of talking beasts.

But we need to know that the world of Narnia did not start off with such a cynical tone. In fact, Uncle Andrew stands in stark contrast to the whole opening scene of chapter 10, where Aslan creates the talking creatures of Narnia. Among the first conversations with these newly made creatures, the first funny thing is said. As a result, all the creatures try to repress their laughter, fearing that everything is supposed to be serious. They do not yet know how to act around such a great and powerful being

9. Eco, *Art and Beauty*, 92–95.

like Aslan. Yet nothing could be further from what Aslan really wants for them. He tells them to "Laugh and fear not, creatures. Now that you are no longer dumb and witless, you need not always be grave. For jokes as well as justice come in with speech." With this one line Lewis brings out the very meaning of divine leisure. According to Lewis, God does not want us to be without the ability to enjoy his world. Thus, in the story all the creatures "let themselves go" in laughter. In the midst of all the joy, the Jackdaw who had spoken the first funny thing exclaimed, "Aslan! Aslan! Have I made the first joke? Will everybody always be told how I made the first joke?" To this Aslan responded, "'No, little friend . . . You have not *made* the first joke; you have only *been* the first joke.' Then everyone laughed more than ever."[10]

As a side note, this whole scene strikes me as a bit ironic. While there is certainly pain and suffering in the world, there is also peace and laughter. While some prefer to ask how a good and loving God could exist where suffering exists, I want to ask how such a pleasure-filled world could exist if no such being was around to allow us to laugh and love in it. For some the "problem" of suffering challenges the notion of how a good God *could* exist. For others the "problem" of love and laughter ought to challenge the notion of how it could even be possible for a good God *not* to exist. The atheist wants a believer like me to explain how pain, suffering, and evil can exist with a good God around. I would also want him/her to explain how real truth, love, joy, and justice can exist if he is *not* around. In my own mind, I can better explain how evil exists in a world where a good God exists simply because humans were the ones who introduced it. I cannot at all explain how love and truth could exist, however, if there were no good God to be our guiding standard to define it. We sin when we take ourselves too seriously. We love and laugh when we are able to take divine living seriously.

But, getting back to the story, if anyone is to blame for ending the party, it is the cynical skeptic. In the midst of the fun, Aslan had to explain that "For though the world is not five hours old an evil has already entered it."[11] But what sin could have been so bad to make Aslan want to stop the party? It was Uncle Andrew. He had overthought things so much to the point that he could no longer think clearly at all. Even though he

10. Lewis, *Magician's Nephew*, 72.
11. Ibid.

saw the miracles with his own eyes and could hear it all with his own ears, he refused to believe any of it was happening.[12] Thus, the first sin in Narnia was the sin of failing to experience divine *leisure*. Uncle Andrew could not laugh because he could not believe. In Aslan's words, it was his failure to allow "jokes as well as justice to come in with speech." Uncle Andrew had refused to accept the existence of divine speech in any form, let alone to participate in divine laughter. What he should have known was that *true* contemplation would never suck divine joy out of living. In fact, it is the only thing that can really allow us to *rest* in the very best sense of the word. But sin and unbelief will ruin your party by making you think and work too hard at the wrong kinds of things and in the wrong kinds of ways. Uncle Andrew had studied Aslan's creation without allowing himself the ability to take in the divine life by accepting the miraculous nature of the scene. He was all work and no play, and, because of this, the greatest thing about his humanity was compromised. He refused to play and laugh with talking beasts because he did not think they could exist. And because of that, Uncle Andrew's view of the world was way too small. And when your world is too small, there is very little room to dance in it. Seen this way, leisure can effectively serve to point us to the divine life. It seems to be no accident, then, that the prodigal son, after quitting his job in the pigpen, was greeted by his father with "music and dancing" when he came back home (Luke 15:25).

12. Ibid., 75.

PART 4

Concerning the Conclusion
of the Argument from Desire

Introduction

THE CONCLUSION OF THE Argument from Desire as adapted from Appendix A of Peter Kreeft's book *Heaven* basically reads as follows: therefore there exists something outside of time and the universe that can satisfy that desire (and the best candidate for that which exists outside of time and the universe is God).[1] In part 4 of this book we dedicate our time to seeing if this conclusion can be substantiated. For if one accepts the first two premises, then the conclusion follows that our unsatisfied desire must come from a source outside of this material universe. However one defines the word "God," it is natural to identify this transcendent source with this term. Of course, what is being suggested here is that the transcendent source for humanity's innate longings is best understood as the same God that C. S Lewis believed would be the final end of his entire search for Joy. But before making this jump, we need to consider at least one more objection to the Argument from Desire.

Thus, the final objection(s) concerns the conclusion itself. Even if we were to grant that all natural desires have objects of some kind that satisfy them (i.e., premise 1), and even if Lewis's divine longing is a natural desire that has no object that satisfies it on earth (i.e., premise 2), it still remains to be seen what kind of object actually exists that serves to satisfy this longing. Perhaps, contrary to anything like theism, evolutionary psychologists and scientists have found a more plausible object to satisfy humanity's desire. Perhaps the object of Lewis's unsatisfied desire is an illusion created in the human brain to make us behave or to give us comfort in the face of annihilation after death.

In what follows we will discuss these objections and attempt to counter them. We believe these objections, while offering seeming plausible answers, ultimately fail in the face of the more robust and stronger case for theism.

---

1. Kreeft, *Heaven*, 202.

Chapter 14

The Evolutionary Objection

To RETURN TO OUR original comparisons between Freud and Lewis discussed in the introduction of this book, what if the theory of evolution is found to be a defeater to the conclusion of the Argument from Desire? As stated in the introduction of part 2 of this book, because John Beversluis does not believe that Joy is a natural desire, he never stopped to consider this important objection that could be raised against this argument. Even if one were to grant that Joy is a natural desire, why not simply say that evolution gave us this sense of transcendent longing so as to give us comfort and security as Freud believed?

Alper's Claim that Religion is Created from a Fear of Extinction

Matthew Alper is one who defends the idea that belief is an evolutionary invention evolved to counter humanity's fear of annihilation in death. He asserts, "Rather than allowing . . . fears to overwhelm and destroy us, perhaps nature selected those whose cognitive sensibilities compelled them to process their concept of death in an entirely new fashion . . . Perhaps a series of neurological connections emerged in our species that compelled us to perceive ourselves as spiritually eternal."[1] He earlier stated that,

> If belief in God is produced by a genetically inherited trait, if the human species is "hardwired" to believe in a spirit world, this could suggest that God doesn't exist as something "out there," beyond and independent of us, but rather as the product of an inherited perception, the manifestation of an evolutionary adaptation that

1. Alper, *Part*, 106.

exists exclusively within the human brain. If true, this would imply that there is no actual spiritual reality, no God or gods, no soul, no afterlife. Consequently, humankind can no longer be viewed as a product of God but rather God must be viewed as a product of human cognition.[2]

An immediate question arises in regard to Alper's point, however. Why would it follow that there would be no God if human beings are hardwired to believe in him? It could just as likely be that, if God exists, he would make beings like us in such a way as to have an innate tendency to believe in him. As Taliaferro comments, "There is no plausible way (I suggest) to move from belief in or experience of X is hard-wired into our brain to X does not (or probably does not) exist. We may be hard-wired to undertake mathematics, to believe there is food and so on. We may be hard-wired to believe in many true things."[3]

How Alper's Claim Fails to Defeat the Argument from Desire

In order for an argument to be either disproven or unfounded there must be some counter argument that serves as a *defeater* to that argument. But there are two different kinds of defeaters to an argument. In order for a counter-argument to serve as a defeater for another argument, it must either be a *rebutting* defeater or an *undercutting* defeater. A rebutting defeater happens when the conclusion of an argument is itself shown to be false. An undercutting defeater happens when the basis or reasons for the conclusion of an argument does not support that conclusion. In a rebutting defeater the opponent affirms the opposite of the conclusion. In an undercutting defeater the opponent claims that the reasons for holding a conclusion are unfounded. In other words, an undercutting defeater does not prove a conclusion false. It merely undermines the basis for which a person holds the conclusion. This distinction is important because Alper seems to be attempting to offer an *undercutting* defeater for theism. He seems to claim that the only reason we believe in God is due to mental processes of the brain. But even if he succeeds in his argument, this proves nothing of whether or not God exists in reality. It would only *undercut* (or undermine) our *reasons* for believing that God exists. But I do not believe

2 Ibid., 79.
3. Taliaferro, "Defense," 103.

that Alper has succeeded in even producing an undercutting defeater against theism. It simply does not follow that, even if the brain does produce belief in God, that this somehow undermines our warrant to believe in him. The human brain may very well produce the belief that we are hungry, but this in no way undercuts the truthfulness of man's need to eat real food. Thus Alper's evolutionary objection does not succeed in either producing a rebutting or an undercutting defeater to the Argument from Desire. We may very well be evolved with a tendency to believe in God or gods, but this still does not explain *why* we might be.

As stated above, similar to many naturalist evolutionary psychologists, Alper seems to assume that God is a made up being that serves as a survival tool to alleviate humanity's fear of annihilation at death. But this objection is weakened, however, by the fact that it cannot be universalized across all human cultures. It narrowly applies to Western ideas about God. In the East, rather than fear death, many religions view the loss of individual personhood (not necessarily annihilation) after death as something to look forward to. Additionally, rather than *creating* an afterlife, cross-cultural studies could equally support the idea that an afterlife of some kind has been *assumed* among ancient humans. Beauregard and O'Leary make this very point regarding Alper's view:

> Alper makes the curious assumption, widespread among atheists, that the origin of belief in God among our ancestors is a desire to survive death. But from what we know, most human cultures have simply assumed that humans survive death. Some hope for heavens, some fear hells, and many anticipate living graveyards or endless rebirths in an unknown state. Indeed, in some religious systems an annihilation desperately sought by the believer cannot be achieved until a high state of spiritual enlightenment has been reached, perhaps through many lives! Far from fearing that souls will simply die, aboriginal cultures in historical times have assumed that the soul is easily detachable from the live body . . .[4]

Thus, even if we were to grant Alper's evolutionary objection, it would not follow that God does not exist. But how else could we show this?

It may be best to answer his evolutionary objection abductively. With this approach we basically ask which alternative makes the most sense given the data we currently have. Paul Copan explains this approach,

---

4. Beauregard and O'Leary, *Brain*, 45–46.

saying, "If an explanation is even remotely logically possible, this does not mean it is just as reasonable as any other. In everyday life, we typically do—and should—prefer explanations that are the most likely or probable, not whatever is merely logically possible."[5]

Even if we allow that evolution explains the natural tendency toward the belief in a transcendent being we are still left to figure out what the best explanation is as to *why* it should be this way. After all, as Swinburne reminds us, "Natural selection is a theory of elimination; it explains why so many of the variants thrown up by evolution were eliminated—they were not fitted for survival. But it does not explain why they were thrown up in the first place."[6]

Consequently, why would blind natural selection favor a longing for something that has never existed? Why would blind natural law give us a natural desire that nothing in nature can satisfy? To ask it this way: what would be the *sufficient* cause of a natural and universal belief in an unnatural, never-existing object? Of course, evolutionary naturalists have a few plausible ways they can answer this that we will discuss below.

Yet in discussing a similar question, Copan considers why moral "values," according to some, could arise from "valueless" processes.[7] He asks, "Doesn't it make more sense to hold that values are rooted in a supremely valuable Being? Value comes from value—not valuelessness."[8]

Borrowing from Copan's question, we could also ask why a longing for an otherworldly being should arise from a non-otherworldly process. Doesn't it make more sense to hold that a sense of the transcendence comes from a transcendent being?

So we go back to our previous point. While evolution might explain the *mechanism* for the biological cause of such a desire, it does not explain *why* such a mechanism should be there to cause the desire in the first place. Thus, we ask, which is the *better* explanation for this unsatisfied longing? Guided, purposeful evolution (i.e., something like theistic evolution), or blind, aimless evolution (i.e., something like naturalistic evolution)?

---

5. Copan, "Naturalists," 51.
6. Swinburne, *Existence*, 207.
7. Copan, "Naturalists," 56.
8. Ibid.

If we answer that unguided, aimless evolution gave us this desire, we should then ask why a blind natural law would give us a natural desire that nothing within nature can satisfy. What would be the sufficient reason for the evolution of a natural, universal belief in an unnatural, never-existing object like God?

If it is just to make us feel better (i.e., to gain a sense of security) as Freud and Alper suggest, then it is not a *necessary* tool for survival. But if it is not necessary for survival, then why would it be necessary for anything at all? Animals seem to live satisfactorily without it. It seems that the desire for the divine has motivated people to accomplish many tasks that fall outside the role of mere survival. Have humans outsmarted blind evolution by evolving a brain that thinks beyond the natural world? Have we now gone beyond mere survival to obtaining a broader flourishing life? Perhaps this is so. But whatever the case, it seems humans believe in the divine for reasons well beyond the mere fear of death. These beliefs, as a matter of fact, provide humanity with much more than a mere defense against fear of extinction.

Richard Dawkins and His Theory of the Accidental Evolution of Divine Desire

But perhaps there is a more robust explanation for the evolution of religious belief. Richard Dawkins offers one plausible account. He admits that religion serves no biological survival purpose directly, but suggests that, "When asked about the survival value of anything, we may be asking the wrong question. We need to rewrite the question in a more helpful way. Perhaps the feature we are interested in (religion in this case) doesn't have a direct survival value of its own, but is a by-product of something that does."[9]

Dawkins holds that religious belief is an unfortunate by-product of a necessary survival tool in children. "Natural Selection builds child brains with a tendency to believe whatever their parents and tribal leaders tell them. Such trusting obedience is valuable for survival."[10] The problem, according to Dawkins, is that the inevitable "flip side" to needed trust is "slavish gullibility." Children need to believe their parents when they tell

9. Dawkins, *Delusion*, 200.
10. Ibid., 205.

them that swimming in crocodile infested rivers is dangerous even if they do not fully understand why. This trust in parental guidance is needed for survival. However, those same children are likely to believe those same parents when they tell them that Santa Claus is real or that sacrificing a goat "at the time of the full moon, otherwise the rains will fail."[11] Seen in this way, one might understand how evolution may have produced a longing for fictitious gods such as the kind of longing Lewis proposed. Simply put, we come into this world with gullible brains.

Why Dawkins's Theory Fails to Defeat the Argument from Desire

However, while Dawkins's view makes sense out of much of the data and shares some degree of plausibility, it does not answer all the necessary questions. For instance, while the *cycle* of the true or false information (say, religious belief or that Santa Clause is real) from generation to generation is explained in Dawkins's theory, it still does not answer why the *content* of the information itself should arise in the first place. We can trace where the tradition of Santa Clause began. Adults intentionally created the story for Christmas time. But where does the notion of a transcendent world come from, and why did it arise? While Dawkins's view might explain some versions of specific religious beliefs and practices located in time, it does not fully explain *why* religious beliefs *per se* should exist in the first place. The child might be gullible to believe that a sacrifice during a full moon will bring rain, but why do the parents believe it? According to Dawkins, it is because their parents told them the same story. But why did *their* parents believe the story? It is because their parents or tribal leaders, in turn, told them, and so on. But once we get to the beginning of the cycle (whenever that might be) we are still left with the same question. *Why* did religious desire and belief arise in the first place?

More importantly, Dawkins's evolutionary objection does not give us any criteria to *determine* which beliefs are true and which beliefs are nonsense. He seems to assume that religious belief is in the category of nonsense. However, this point begs the question. He is right to point out the gullibility (or trusting nature) of the child brain. But this says nothing about the truth-value of certain propositions themselves. Say, for instance,

11. Ibid.

that we did live in a world where there was a godlike being who would send rain if the people he created would offer a full-moon-time sacrifice. Such a world is not a logical impossibility. Or say that we lived in a world where crocodiles were as harmless as goldfish. While the proposition "Swimming in crocodile infested rivers is dangerous" might be true in this world, it could have been false in another one. In this world it is true, but in the other possible world the proposition would be nonsense. Thus, Dawkins does not provide any kind of fatal explanation against theism. His view, at best, would only prove that children are gullible to believe both true and false propositions. But we still are left to determine which propositions are true and which ones are not.

Contrary to Dawkins, we could just as well assert that, rather than being an unfortunate by-product of some other necessary survival mechanism, belief in God is actually evidence that God does, in fact, exist. Just as evolution (in whatever form) has produced a true belief that swimming in crocodile infested waters is dangerous, it just as likely could have produce a true belief in a God who began the evolutionary process to begin with. Thus we are back to our original question. If evolution has given us an instinct that moves us past survival to a broader, imaginative, and flourishing life (including the notion of *eternal* life), then which version of evolution makes better sense: a blind, unguided, unimaginative evolution; or an intelligent, imaginatively guided one?

It seems less likely to me that a blind and aimless evolution is going to make us look or move past our empirical situation toward the belief in a non-empirical fictitious world of gods and ghosts. If a finch, for example, has a beak that is uniquely shaped to allow him to get the insects out of certain kinds of trees, it's only because those trees were there to begin with. It seems that with the desire for transcendence (call it God or eternal life), humanity has outsmarted *blind* evolution if there is nothing that exists in nature to cause us to evolve a desire for something *supernatural*. If the only function of natural selection, strictly speaking, is to blindly remove the species that does not have the needed mechanisms for survival, what has caused humans to look beyond the stars if we can live just fine within them? The fact that we do look beyond them seems, in my view, to support an "intelligent" (or goal-directed) form of evolution more so than blind (non-directed) evolution. But why should I think this?

Put it this way: If God exists and has made humanity for a relationship with him, then would we not expect to find a desire in mankind that finds no earthly satisfaction? Since we do find such a desire, does this not verify the above assumption in a world where God would exist? In other words, if a relational God does exist, we would expect to find beings who have a desire for him just like the kind of desire we do, in fact, find us having.

On the other hand, what if we posed the question in the other direction? If a blind (goal-less) evolution is true, would we expect to find a made-up, imaginary, non-existent heavenly Being to evolve in the minds of beings to satisfy a natural earthly need for security (as Freud and Alper suppose)? Or (as Dawkins suggests) is belief in God merely a gullible by-product of some other survival mechanism?

Even if the answer to the latter two questions could *logically* be yes, is it a more *plausible* answer given the previous possibility? It seems to me, that an intelligently guided evolutionary process, say, by a divine Being, would make more explanatory sense for this desire than an unguided one. Copan offered an insightful comment on this point when he said,

> Removing God from the metaphysical picture means eliminating significant explanatory power for a wide range of phenomena. Consider which context—naturalism or theism—has the greater ring of plausibility for the following features of the universe: That consciousness came from non-conscious matter or from a supremely self-aware Being? That personhood emerged through impersonal processes or by way of a personal Creator? That free will / personal responsibility emerged from deterministic processes or from a being or personal agent who freely chose to create? That the universe just popped into existence, uncaused, from nothing, a finite time ago out of nothing or that a powerful being brought it into existence? That the universe happened to be staggeringly precise for biological life or that a transcendent intelligence is responsible? These phenomena serve as indicators of transcendence, pointing to an ontologically haunted universe.[12]

It seems to me that Copan's thoughts are equally applicable to the Argument from Desire. Thus it is at least reasonable to say that "God (or something like him/it) exists" is the most likely conclusion given the entirety of the Argument from Desire and the greater explanatory power that it confers.

---

12. Copan, "Naturalists," 56.

Putting It All Together: Why the Evolutionary Objection Can Never Disprove Theism

It is difficult to overcome the combination of Copan's argument of the explanatory power of theism with Plantinga's view (described above) that properly working human cognitive faculties (such as intentionality, memory, and rationality) are truth-aimed and that we generally assume that these faculties are reliable. If such arguments are not sound, how then can we account for the broadly held belief of some kind of supernatural reality if it is found to be untrue?

Richard Swinburne defended two principles that are additionally helpful here. He affirmed a principle known as the "principle of credulity." This view states that things should generally be believed to be the way they appear to be unless there is some clear and compelling reason to think otherwise. He words this principle thus:

> I suggest that it is a principle of rationality that (in the absence of special considerations), if it seems (epistemically) to a subject that x is present (and has some characteristic), then probably x is present (and has that characteristic); what one seems to perceive is probably so.[13]

Swinburne's other principle is called the "principle of testimony." This principle states that we ought to believe what *other* people tell us when they say that things are the way they seem to them unless there is some compelling reason to believe otherwise.[14] If we apply Plantinga's point with Swinburne's principles we will be more inclined to think that something like theism is true. Note the following argument:

1. It seems that most humans believe that something like a transcendent reality exists beyond the material world.

2. Human cognitive faculties (such as intentionality, rationality, and memory) tend to be truth-aimed and reliable if working properly.

3. But if properly working human cognitive faculties (such as described in premise 2) tend to be truth-aimed and reliable, then the broad belief that something like a transcendent reality (as affirmed in premise 1) ought to be thought of as true.

13. Swinburne, *Existence*, 303.
14. Ibid., 322–23.

4. Therefore it is more rational to believe that something like a transcendent reality probably exists beyond the material world than not to believe.

Thus we submit, even granting the basis for the evolutionary objection, that, between the explanatory power outlined by Copan, combined with a Reidian-like common sense approach of Plantinga and Swinburne, an evolution that is guided by a supernatural or intelligent process that is goal-directed stands as the most plausible view. Consequently, since we have a desire for transcendence, it would follow that the supernatural being that is responsible for evolution would also be responsible for Lewis's natural desire for the divine. Therefore, desire for an object (supernatural being) that is not part of this world indeed points us to, and serves as evidence for, that supernatural being, even if we, again, were to grant Darwinian evolutionary assumptions of natural selection.

Chapter 15

Is There a Human Gene For *Sehnsucht*?

IN CONNECTION TO THE points made in the previous chapter, one of the big debates within evolutionary science is the question concerning whether humans possess something like a "God gene." To phrase this issue for our purposes: If C. S. Lewis's idea of longing for God (i.e., Joy or *Sehnsucht*) is truly a natural one, might we simply explain this phenomenon as a mere product of our inherited genes? If so, does this undercut the conclusion that God must exist to serve as the object that satisfies this longing?

Michael Murray and the "God Gene"

Professor Michael Murray makes many observations that are helpful in trying to answer this question. "Humans come into the world with all sorts of 'software' both preinstalled and booted up. Some of this software manifests itself right from birth, while other bits of it become operative at specifiable times in human development."[1] One way we can look for beliefs that arise from built-in "software" is to look for "Beliefs that are pervasive across times and cultures." Some beliefs are held because of external evidence. However, other, "Beliefs seem to arise despite an absence of sufficient sensory evidence. Such beliefs are said to arise despite a 'poverty of the stimulus,' and when such beliefs occur, we have reason to look for built-in, onboard processing mechanisms that provide what our experiences do not.[2]

Examples Murray gives are the belief that rotting food, corpses, and animal waste are dangerous. He goes on to say, "This set of beliefs and the

1. Murray, "Belief," 47.
2. Ibid., 49.

accompanying desires, known in psychology as 'contagion avoidance,' is found across cultures, even in cases where people have little or no direct evidence for its truth. We are, it seems, wired to believe it.[3]

This does not mean that the content of knowledge itself is innate. Murray is not suggesting that one knows *who* God is at birth, but only that our genes dispose us toward belief in God. It is more like what Alvin Plantinga suggests when he says, "The *capacity* for such knowledge is indeed innate."[4] Thus, the second premise of the Argument from Desire does not imply anything like Plato's pre-existence of souls. It simply states that we do in fact have an innate tendency and capacity for this divine desire.

And yet, as long as we can reach back into time humanity has had this desire to worship transcendent objects, persons, or gods. While far from having all the answers, the field of neuroscience is now learning more about some of the reasons why human beings are so spiritual. The interesting thing is that what they have to say is very consistent with what C. S. Lewis says in his Argument from Desire. What both modern scientists and Lewis suggest in their own ways is that the tendency to believe in the divine is hardwired into our brain, at least in some sense.

According to Murray, there are many evolutionary and cognitive explanations for the idea that "aim to show that human beings are naturally disposed toward religious belief."[5] Some of the evidences are quite fascinating. First, there is the "Hyperactive Agency Detection Device" (or "HADD"). This human mental tool allows us to "hypothesize invisible agents that, for example, control the forces of nature."[6] One can thus imagine invisible and powerful agents working beyond the natural realm causing things to happen on a cosmic scale.

Second, because these ideas are so strange to the external world we tend to remember and talk about them, and "this makes these religious concepts spread rapidly from mind to mind." In this way, individual as well as communal religious desire comes naturally from both the biological as well as a social point of view. Working with our natural tendencies to believe, tradition becomes a powerful force.

---

3. Ibid.
4. Plantinga, *Belief*, 173.
5. Murray, "Belief," 51.
6. Ibid., 52.

Third, according to Murray, "There is strong evidence that we are naturally disposed from an early age to see *goal-directedness* in everything."[7] Cognitive theorists call this tendency "intuitive theism" or "natural teleology." One of the reasons the teleological argument appeals to so many is because this is the natural way of thinking of the world. We are almost forced to think in terms of goal-directed laws in both human nature and the world.

Aristotle's Eudaimonia (i.e., Ultimate Happiness) and Its Potential Relationship to Lewis's Sehnsucht (i.e., Divine Longing)

Of course, Aristotle taught us all this well before modern science did. He taught that everything that contained both matter plus form had its own designed *telos* (or goal). This included the human being as a rational animal.

According to Aristotle, matter does not just refer to the physical property of a thing itself. Matter for Aristotle (and later Aquinas) refers to *potential* identity. The *form* of an object is the *actualization* of that matter into the thing it becomes. If the *matter* of a thing is its possible existence and its potential identity, the *form* of the thing is its actual existence and its defining characteristic (i.e., the *form* gives *existence* to *matter* and *identity*). A biological body alone might exist as a physical thing, but it is does not yet exist as a human body. It is only the *soul* of man that makes a person's body a *human* body. Without the soul, the body is only potentially human (i.e., matter). But with the soul it is actually human (i.e., form). Thus, the soul is the very form of the body. As its form, the human soul is the source of the person's rational life and its defining characteristic (i.e., activity). The body is a human body that grows, thinks, learns, and loves precisely because it has a soul.[8]

Consequently, for Aristotle, order must have an unmoved, ordering source.[9] Thus, the human being (i.e., the composite of both matter and rational soul) has a divine *telos* that is geared for man's *eudaimonia*.[10]

---

7. Ibid.
8. Aristotle, *Metaphysics*, 119–42.
9. Ibid., 242.
10. Aristotle, *Nicomachean Ethics*, 1–21.

While this word is often translated "happiness" in Aristotle, *eudaimonia* is better understood to refer to the "flourishing" of the human being in accord with what he was designed for as a rational animal. Virtue and reason were two of the foundations of this human *telos*. Thus, it is within the nature of a human being to live his/her life toward this rational and virtuous goal. Thus virtue, for Aristotle, was found in the doer and not merely in the deed done. We bring all this up now to say that, for Aristotle, this virtuous *telos* was innate and tied directly to the divine purpose of humanity's existence. As he said in his *Ethics*,

> But if the happiness is being-at-work in accord with virtue, it is reasonable that it would belong to the best part. Now whether this is intellect or some other part that seems by nature to rule and lead and have a conception about things that are beautiful and divine, and to be either divine itself or the most divine of the things in us, the being-at-work of this part in accord with its own proper virtue would be complete happiness.[11]

Thus humanity's "own proper virtue" (i.e., what it is designed for) will produce in itself the goal of happiness since it seems "by nature" to rule and lead it to things that are "beautiful and divine." This just appears to be another way of getting at what in people is driving Lewis's *Sehnsucht*.

Consequently, the similarities of *Sehnsucht* and *eudaimonia* seem compelling. Both are only fully attained at the end of life,[12] and both are expressed as a never-ending search for our true destiny (*telos*), which is never fully satisfied on earth. The difference is that, according to some readings of Aristotle, what continues after death may be the intellect, at least, in some form, but for Lewis it is the whole human being in the resurrection. At bare minimum, Aristotle looked to gain a legacy of human virtue at the end of life. Lewis looked to gain a life of salvation.

But returning to Murray's argument, this goal-directedness is more concretely understood to dispose us to believe in a purpose-giving force in the universe, that is, to believe in gods or a God.

Murray tells us of an experiment by Jesse Bering that showed that even at an early age children tend to follow rules more consistently when they believe that a supernatural agent is watching them.

---

11. Ibid., 191.
12. Ibid., 14–17.

Is There a Human Gene For Sehnsucht?

In one experiment subjects were brought into a room and shown a box under two conditions. In one condition the child is told that there is an invisible princess in the room named Alice, who is carefully watching the whole experiment. In the control condition children are not told any story about Alice. The children were then told that inside the box was a special prize and that they could have the prize only if they could guess what it was without looking. After giving the child the instructions, the experimenter tells the child that he needs to step out of the room for the moment. Children who had received the Alice prime cheated significantly less than those who did not, and even among cheaters it took much longer for primed subjects to cheat than subjects who were not primed.[13]

According to Murray, evidence indicates the same effects for adults. Clearly this experiment shows that children have a natural tendency to believe. It also happens to show, contrary to some, that religion serves a helpful and useful role in morality in society.

But does all this show that religion is simply a "trick of the brain"? Some have looked at evidence such as that shown above and concluded that "God is an artifact of the brain." Murray quotes Bering as saying that "we've got God by the throat and I'm not going to stop until one of us is dead."[14]

It seems that those, like Alper and Bering, who, on evidence such as the experiment described above, have concluded that God does not exist, have committed an obvious fallacy. As stated above, and as Murray also argues, it seems that they are thinking that if the development of the human mind produces belief in the gods, then the gods cannot be real. If so, then they are committing a typical genetic fallacy. They are claiming that belief in God is wrong simply because of where the belief originates. But just because a belief comes from a source that may or may not be objectively reliable does not mean that the belief itself is false. If such is the case, then Freud and Nietzsche were right all along. But if this is not the case, then they prove nothing about the truth-value of faith.

Take, for example, that a person believes the next lucky lotto numbers are going to be 3, 9, 19, 21, 23, and 27 because these are the numbers of all his/her family members' birthdays. Can someone claim that these

13. Murray, "Belief," 53.
14. Ibid., 54.

numbers are wrong just because the numbers are selected in an unusual way? Obviously this is not the case. "It may be true, despite the strange origin."[15]

"But," Murray considers, "maybe" the belief is simply not warranted. Who would argue that one is warranted to believe that those numbers would be the lucky lotto numbers simply because of the way they were selected?

This is where belief in God is different from our lotto illustration. There was no natural link between the numbers and the lotto drawing. This is not true for belief in God. If we (adapting Murray's point) take the phrase "Since the development of human minds has produced belief in god, belief in god is false," then what do we find? Are we without warrant to believe in God just because we have come to that belief through our own natural cognitive faculties, without further formal evidence?

As Murray points out, what if one were to replace the name "god" for "human minds" or "the past"? How would the statement sound then? It would say, "Since the development of human minds has produced belief that other people have conscious minds, belief in other minds is false." Is one without warrant to believe in other minds just because they may not have further formal arguments to prove it?

Or consider this statement. "Since the faculties of your own mind have produced the belief that there is such a thing as a past, belief in the past is false." Is a person unwarranted to believe in the past just because the past cannot be demonstrated through formal argumentation? If someone tried to prove to you that he/she had a past how would he/she go about doing that? The person could just tell you about it. But how do you know the person is not making it all up? How do you know that your own past history was not planted there five minutes ago by space aliens or by an evil Cartesian demon?

The fact is that a person is warranted to believe certain properly basic propositions even without absolute formal proof. Now you know why our introduction to these matters in chapter 3 was so critical to Lewis's argument. This is how the Argument from Desire works. A person is warranted in believing that their unsatisfied longing for transcendence (i.e., *Sehnsucht*) is satisfied by a loving God simply because it is properly basic to their generally reliable cognitive faculties and tendencies to do so. One

---

15. Ibid., 55.

cannot prove this argument through empirical deduction *alone* (thus the attempt was made to demonstrate *hints* or *echoes* of it inductively in part 3). We believe the conclusion is *prima facie* rational, nonetheless. We believe that it makes the best sense out of the data we have, out of what we find in the world and what we find in our souls.

Pascal and Intuitive Faith

But in addition to Aristotle and Lewis, Murray is saying what the French mathematician and philosopher Blaise Pascal once said as well: "We know the truth not only by means of reason but also by means of the heart. It is through the heart that we know the first principles . . . We know that we are not dreaming, however powerless we are to prove it by reason. This powerlessness proves only the weakness of our reason, not the uncertainty of our entire knowledge as they claim."[16]

By "heart" Pascal means intuition. But by intuition he does not mean whatever is "irrational." Intuition is whatever is rationally accepted through natural phenomenon that is immediate, personal, and direct, as opposed to what is proved and calculated. The "heart" for Pascal is what Murray means by "built-in, onboard processing mechanisms." This serves as the basis for Lewis's *Sehnsucht*. The external world serves as the signpost to faith, while divine desire serves as a kind of natural triggering mechanism. As Williams explains, "It might be that need is acting not as an element in an evidential argument, but as a triggering condition for belief. A triggering condition is an event or state that produces a belief without going through an inferential process. The belief is caused by the event; one does not construct an argument for the belief."[17]

Williams goes on to give an illustration of what he means by a "triggering condition" (i.e., what one would call "intuition").

> The argument from design for believing in God says that the universe must have a maker because the ordered complexity in it requires a maker Here complexity, or the belief in complexity, operates as a part of a reasoning process, short though it may be. If however, the complexity (or the belief in complexity) were acting as a triggering condition, it would simply cause the belief

16. Pascal, *Pensees*, 35.
17. Williams, *Reasons*, 68

in a cosmic designer without going through the reasoning process. The belief in a cosmic designer would be evoked by the complexity immediately without the intervening premise that complexity requires a designer.[18]

This is a good illustration of what Pascal means by contrasting the terms "heart" and "reason." By "reason" he does not mean rationality, but formal argumentation. By "heart" he does not mean irrationality, but rather a way of knowing what is intimate, immediate, and natural to our being.

This makes sense in a Christian worldview because, according to what Pascal and Murray have said, humans are not just called to know *about* God. They are called to *know* God. A person does not just know about his/her loved ones, he/she knows them personally and directly. Reason is what people use to know about someone. The heart is what they use to know them personally and intimately. But the heart does not just *know*, it also *sees* and *understands*. It is the deep part of who we are that transcends mere intellectual informational gathering. It is the part of us who takes the information we know through intuition and reason, makes sense of it, and then decides how to feel about it. The heart then motivates us concerning what to *do* about what we know. Acting in this role, the heart can also be understood as the seat of the human will.

But while our faith in God is natural, it is not inevitable. Again as Pascal says, "I say that it is natural for the heart to love the universal being or itself, according to its allegiance, and it hardens itself against either as it chooses."[19] And foreshadowing the language of Lewis's *Sehnsucht*, Pascal proclaims, "It is a monstrous thing to see one and the same heart at once so sensitive to minor things and so strangely insensitive to the greatest. It is an incomprehensible spell, a supernatural torpor that points to an omnipotent power as its cause."[20]

18. Ibid., 68–69.
19. Kreeft, *Christianity*, 231.
20. Ibid., 194.

Conclusion

The Argument from Desire does not prove that God exists, let alone does it *prove* that the God of Christian theism exists. What it seeks to show is that it is rational to believe that something must exist that is beyond this world and that gives us a sense of longing for it. Call it eternal life; call it heaven; or call it God. The one thing that seems most certain is that we all have a longing that is never satisfied in this world. And since all other innate desires have something that satisfies those desires, there must be something or someone that exists to satisfy this desire, too.

Though it is not proven, we believe the best and most probable candidate to fulfill this longing (aching) that we have is in fact God. The case for this conclusion is best understood as an inductive one. It is, we believe, a very strong argument. But it is nothing like a deductive case that fulfills anything like Cartesian certainty.

The Cumulative Case for God and How the Argument from Desire Fits into It

Additionally, as in all the arguments for divine existence it is best looked at in the context of the cumulative case. Like the Cosmological Argument, the Argument from Design feels natural to us. People often look out at the stars and ask, "How could this get here without intelligent causes?" They look into their hearts and ask, "How could we feel this way if there is no one out there to have given us this ability to feel?" They are told by many that evolution explains it all. Yet human nature still longs for more. Why should the beautiful portrait of a mountain, but not the real thing, need a painter? Why do human beings throughout all time and cultures get the feeling they're being watched by an eye that is bigger than the sky above us? Of course we are now being told not to trust our feelings. Feelings can deceive. This is true.

Conclusion

And yet, since they are such a part of human nature, feelings do have a place in intellectual discussion. Feelings do not always mean the same thing as emotion. By "feelings" it is sometimes meant simply an inner sense of what appears rational *res ipsa loquitur* (i.e., the thing speaks for itself). It is like what Pascal wrote when he said, "the heart has reasons that reason knows nothing of."[1] As discussed above, he did not mean by this that emotions should be trusted more than the intellect. He was suggesting to us that human beings have an inner sense that is itself rational. It is like having a piece of an environmental puzzle (i.e., it just fits). These feelings, when mixed with natural and universal needs in a conducive environment, can have a great deal to say to us. Parents know this feeling when their child has done something wrong but they do not know quite what it is. Experienced police officers get this feeling when faced with a person that has done something criminal but they have no formal evidence for it. This intuition indeed has a place in intellectual discussion. The Argument from Desire is best seen not only within the context of the cumulative case for God's existence. It also serves to verify what we already feel deep down in our "gut." We are not alone in this world. There is a Holy Presence that (or rather "who") also serves as the reason why any of us are here in the first place.

Reepicheep's Personal Argument from Desire

To keep this work focused we have intentionally and primarily limited ourselves to the non-fictional works of C. S. Lewis when discussing his presentation of the argument. But this longing for transcendence is found all through his works of fiction as well. Some of the best comes from his *Till We Have Faces*, *The Chronicles of Narnia*, *The Pilgrim's Regress*, and the *Space Trilogy*. But to illustrate what we have been talking about we will close by looking at one famous case of *Sehnsucht* in C. S. Lewis's work *The Voyage of the Dawn Treader*. In this story there is a mouse named Reepicheep who has become one of the more famous and lovable characters in the *Chronicles of Narnia* series.

In the book, Reepicheep accompanies Caspian and friends on a long and adventurous journey. But while Reepicheep is on this journey to

---

1 Kreeft, *Christianity*, 231.

assist the companions in the mission to find the seven lost lords, he has a "higher hope" that has haunted him all his life.

As they were discussing what sort of country Aslan's would be and where it could be found, Lucy asked,

> "'But do you think,' said Lucy, 'Aslan's country would be that sort of country—I mean, the sort you could ever sail to?'

'I do not know, Madam,' said Reepicheep. 'But there is this. When I was in my cradle, a wood woman, a Dryad, spoke this verse over me:

> Where sky and water meet,
> Where the waves grow sweet,
> Doubt not, Reepicheep,
> To find all you seek,
> There is the utter east.
>
> I do not know what it means.
> But the spell of it has been on me all my life.'"[2]

It is "Aslan's country" that has kept Reepicheep in a lifelong spell. He would later say that it is his very "heart's desire."[3] This is Reepicheep's own personal Argument from Desire. Like Reepicheep, it is as if we are also under a sort of "spell" that moves us along the adventures of life in hopes of finding the divine.

At the end of the story Reepicheep and friends finally arrive in the east and come to a wave so tall it reaches the sky. It is a wall of water separating them from Aslan's country. No one can make out what is behind the wall but the mystery of it entices them each. As they looked,

> No one in that boat doubted that they were seeing beyond the End of the World into Aslan's country. At that moment, with a crunch, the boat ran aground. The water was too shallow now for it. "This," said Reepicheep "is where I go on alone."
>
> They did not even try to stop him, for everything now felt as if it had been fated or had happened before. They helped him to lower his little coracle. Then he took off his sword ("I shall need it no more", he said) and flung it faraway across the lilied sea . . . then he bade them goodbye, trying to be sad for their sakes; but he was quivering with happiness. Lucy, for the first time and last time, did

2. Lewis, *Voyage*, 433.
3. Ibid., 521.

Conclusion

> what she always wanted to do, taking him in her arms and caressing him. Then hastily he got into his coracle and took his paddle, and the current caught it and away he went, very black against the lilies... The coracle went more and more quickly, and beautifully it rushed up the wave's side. For one split second they saw its shape and Reepicheep's on the very top. Then it vanished, and since that moment no one can truly claim to have seen Reepicheep the Mouse. But my belief is that he came safe to Aslan's country and is alive there to this day.[4]

Reepicheep serves as a great character who reminds us of this deep longing we have. Again, it is not just a feeling. It is a sense of needing and wanting more. It is a spirit of restlessness until we come to the object we crave. But the restlessness we have is itself an adventure. We crave the travels and the journey. We appreciate the beauty around us on the way.

Life's journey of divine yearning is itself a Joy. It is like a search for lost treasure. The treasure may be the goal but it is in the search itself that we find out what we are made of. The mystery and anticipation is the ongoing treasure as we move closer toward the *end treasure*. Lewis would have nothing to do with an escapist view of life. In Lewis's thinking, those who hold that this world is only a transitional phase in which we simply wait for the real thing are mistaken. This world is where we learn how to dance for the long-awaited ball. It is a world where lovers sing until that Joyous song is heard in the chorus of angels. This world is not a waiting room. It is a training room. For Lewis, it is here that we learn of the real Aslan. After Reepicheep takes leave for Aslan's country, Lucy asks Aslan,

> "Will you tell us how to get into your country from our world?"
> "I shall be telling you all the time," said Aslan...
> "It isn't Narnia, you know," sobbed Lucy, "It's you. We shan't meet you there. And how can we live, never meeting you?"
> "But you shall meet me, dear one," said Aslan.
> "Are—are you there too, Sir?" said Edmond.
> "I am," said Aslan. "But there I have another name.
>   You must learn to know me by that name."[5]

At the end of the *Voyage*, Lewis finally offers a clear glimpse into what the real object of human desire is. It is not only heaven. Human longing is not for another world like ours that simply has more things to

---

4. Ibid., 539–40.
5. Ibid., 540–41.

do for fun with a prettier environment. One does not, in fact, long for a place. We long for a *Person*. In the words of the Narnian chronicler, we long for "Aslan" himself. And, as Lewis was creatively hinting at, the name he is known in our world is "Jesus Christ." But Joy *on its own* does not tell us about Jesus. At best it leads us to a God whose definition is somewhat different than Anselm's, yet is related. Anselm defined God positively as "than that which nothing greater can be conceived." The search for the object of Joy might more simply lead us to a God who is defined as "that satisfying Object (or Person) which is more than anything that exists in this universe." Of course Lewis's actual view is much more specific than that. All of his fiction (most notably the *Chronicles of Narnia*) serves not just as "training in how to long"; it also serves to introduce us to "what and whom to long for."[6] To know more about this "whom" we will have to get it from some other source. To know the Jesus that Lewis came to know and love would require a specific kind of knowledge that must come through divine revelation. But that discussion is for another time and another book.

---

6. Jacobs, "Chronicles," 279.

Appendix

The *End* of Human Desire

AUGUSTINE ONCE PRAYED, "You have made us for Yourself and restless is the human heart until it rests in you."[1]

But why is the human heart in such a state of unrest? As we have seen, Lewis believed, as Augustine, that the desire Christians feel carries a heavy burden as well as a joyful hope. But how does one deal with this tension between restlessness and joy. And why does one have it at all? And, more specifically, what does Lewis's *Sehnsucht* tell us about the human state of restlessness and hope?

Remembering Home

One of the Christian teachings is that mankind has fallen from a sinless state in a garden called Eden. The Garden of Eden was home. The original family walked and worked without fear and turmoil (Gen 1–2). Before sin they walked openly in the garden with God speaking with them closely and directly (Gen 1:8). This peaceful home, according to Scripture is clearly where humanity was supposed to dwell. Had mankind never sinned the boundaries of the Garden would have continued to expand throughout the entire world as God had told them even before the Fall to "fill the earth and subdue it" (Gen 1:28–29).

But if the Garden was mankind's original home, then what does one call where we are right now? The Bible gives us a picture that humans are "pilgrims" and "strangers" in a foreign land (1 Pet 2:11). We live in a land that has been altered to the point that it no longer satisfies our nature the

---

1. Augustine, *Confessions*, 11.

way our original home did. What was once originally prepared for us is now something we only dream and read about.

This does not mean that planet Earth was not supposed to be home. But even a superficial reading of Genesis 3 will remind us that sin has changed our world dramatically. While one still sees its wonderful beauties, the creation has now been infected by sin. The restlessness that Augustine spoke of includes the idea that people can have a feeling of homelessness even while living in the very place that was supposed to be called home. In a real way, what Lewis spoke of in *Sehnsucht* would not have existed in the Garden. There would have been no desires left unfulfilled. Humans were originally created in a world where all of their natural desires could be met. God directly communed with Adam and Eve. Of course they would have had a continuous desire for God, but it would have been continuously filled by his immediate and visible presence.

Thus, the unsatisfied desire for transcendence is another way of speaking about our homesickness (or Augustine's "restlessness"). In a sense, it is a human memory of a past we have never seen. This ability to "remember" builds within us the discontentment and frustration found in *Sehnsucht*.

In the usual sense, memory and recollection typically convey the idea of bringing to mind what was once personally experienced by the individual. In this sense, one cannot remember what they have not gone through personally. Plato uses the word recollection to refer to past events that a person's soul went through before entering his body. The pre-existence of the soul is an important feature in Platonic thought.

Thus for Plato, to remember the soul's past home literally meant that the soul could recollect its pre-existent life in the world of the forms before it became embodied.[2] The soul's home was remembered when the mind tapped into the knowledge that was already possessed by the person.

However, memory does not always mean that we are bringing to mind what we ourselves have experienced. Sometimes memory means that we bring to mind something from the past through the experiences of the present that connect us to that past experience. For Christians the Lord's Supper is a case in point.

> For I received from the Lord that which I also delivered to you: that the Lord Jesus on the same night in which He was betrayed

---

2. Plato, "Phaedo," 223–29.

> took bread; and when He had given thanks, He broke it and said, "Take, eat; this is My body which is broken for you; do this in remembrance of Me." In the same manner He also took the cup after supper, saying, "This cup is the new covenant in My blood. This do, as often as you drink it, in remembrance of Me. (Matt 26:26–27.)

Clearly Jesus did not mean that one can "remember" his death in the same way that one remembers getting up this morning. One can remember getting up this morning because one personally experienced the event. Yet how does one remember his death? One remembers it through at least three avenues. First, one remembers it through the traditions that have been handed down through the church. Since the church has practiced and taught about the death of Jesus, we can better know (i.e., "remember") that past event. Second, one remembers it through the physical elements that Jesus (and here Paul) told us to use. The cup is to represent (i.e., to create an image into our minds) the blood of Jesus. The bread is to represent (i.e., to create the image upon our minds) the body that was put on the cross to die. In this way one "remembers" or has an image of the truth in their minds of what took place in the death of Jesus. To "remember" is to also make that past experience somehow our own in the present: to make it applicable to us. Third, Scripture reveals the event of Jesus' death in written form. This gives one the assurance and details to ensure that whatever has been filtered out through tradition is still preserved. Thus through the three present avenues of personal experience a person can "remember" and "experience" the events of the past.

The same way that one can "remember" the death of Jesus, we submit, is the same way that one can "remember" life in the Garden. While no one today has ever been in the Garden of Eden, they can "remember" it through the same three ways that they can remember the death of Jesus.

First, one remembers the Garden through tradition. By tradition we mean the human experience of longing and aching for peace instead of war, and happiness instead of chaos. The fact that we know something horrible has gone wrong in our world tells our hearts that it must have been right before and can be set right again. The human efforts toward justice are witnesses that such a thing really exists and has existed.

Second, one remembers the Garden through the physical elements of all that is beautiful in the world. The reader is asked to recall all that was said in part 3. These elements of imagination, beauty, and leisure

Appendix

communicate to us (i.e., stamps the image upon our hearts) that such a fairy-story world, a colorful beauty, and fullness of life really did exist in our world and will exist again.

Third, one remembers the Garden through Scripture that describes it to us. A quick reading of Genesis 1–3 and Revelation 21–22 will let one know what our hearts are longing for.

Thus, because we remember paradise through these three avenues, and because God has put into our hearts this innate desire for transcendence, these are some of the reasons we experience what Lewis called *Sehnsucht*. We desire to go back to the home we "remember." We are haunted by both a transcendent presence as well as a yearning that one day we will return. In commenting on Plato's idea of remembering, Josef Pieper states that

> "Yearning" and "recollection" point back toward the original state of the beginning, which concurrently appears as the true aim of life . . . the picture of the perfect life which was in the beginning and will be again in the end . . . This then, is what the soul which has fallen, through wickedness and forgetfulness, into the world of corporeal men, remembers . . . and therefore [men] have not lost their memory of an earlier blessed state. One can recover it all when one "stands aside from the busy doings of mankind" and steps forth out of the workaday world.[3]

Plato may have been wrong about the pre-existence of the soul. But his error, we submit, is one of simply going backward too far in time. Modern man can "remember" and, thus, yearn for paradise. But it is not because he has himself been there. In part 3 we learned about many things that press these images into our minds. Yet it is Scripture that can tell more concretely what our souls through *Sehnsucht* has been trying to tell us all along.

To repeat C. S. Lewis who said it best, "All the things that have ever deeply possessed your soul have been but hints of it—tantalizing glimpses, promises never quite fulfilled, echoes that died away just as they caught your ear. But if it should really become manifest—if there even came an echo that did not die away but swelled into the sound itself—you would know it. Beyond all possibility of doubt you would say, "Here at last is the thing I was made for."[4]

3. Pieper, *Enthusiasm & Madness*, 80–81.
4. Lewis, *Problem*, 131.

Appendix

Until then, we wait with earnest desire, a desire that is itself a divine gift while we wait. It is this desire that has inspired poetry, motivated love, created dreams, healed the hopeless, and fueled human progress. In short, it has helped to maintain the humanness of humanity. The Germans could call it *Sehnsucht*. C. S. Lewis called it "Joy." The Bible calls him "Jesus." And one day, according to Paul, he will come to deliver the whole creation and set all things right (Rom 8:18–22). This is the end (i.e., goal) of all human desire.

Sehnsucht: Humanity's Aching for Home

To emphasize the point, again we repeat what Alan Jacobs says about Joy and its connection to sin and salvation. "*Sehnsucht* is the mood of our world: the Silent Planet longs for connection, for restoration of the music of the other spheres from which we have cut ourselves off."[5]

These words remind me of two Christian apologists: One is the first-century apostle Paul and the other is the twenty-first-century singer Laura Story. While Paul reminds us that the whole creation is "groaning" in pain while it "eagerly awaits" for its "deliverance" (Rom 8:18–21), Laura Story reminds us that all this groaning serves a purpose. She musically offers her own form of the Argument from Desire. It comes in the words of her song *Blessings*.

> 'Cause what if Your blessings come through raindrops
> What if Your healing comes through tears?
> And what if a thousand sleepless nights
> Are what it takes to know You're near?
> What if my greatest disappointments
> Or the aching of this life
> Is the revealing of a greater thirst
> This world can't satisfy?
> And what if trials of this life
> The rain, the storms, the hardest nights
> Are Your mercies in disguise?

At the very least, the Argument from Desire forces us to ask that very question: What if? If one is open to the argument's possibilities, one might just get a hauntingly beautiful answer. In the process one may even end up satisfying the heart's deepest desire one day: in the day to end all days.

5. Jacobs, "Chronicles," 278.

Bibliography

Adler, Mortimer. *How to Think about God: A Guide for the 20th-Century Pagan*. New York: Macmillan, 1991.
Alper, Matthew. *The 'God' Part of the Brain: A Scientific Interpretation of Human Spirituality and God*. Naperville, IL: Sourcebooks, 2008.
Aquinas, Thomas. *Summa of the Summa*. Edited and annotated by Peter Kreeft. San Francisco: Ignatius, 1990.
Aristotle. *Metaphysics*. Translated by Joe Sachs. Santa Fe: Green Lion, 2002.
———. *Nicomachean Ethics*. Translated by Joe Sachs. Newburyport, MA: Focus, 2002.
Auden, W. H. *The Dryer's Hand and Other Essays*. New York: Vintage International, 1989.
Augustine. *Confessions*. Alachua, FL: Bridge-Logos, 2003.
Bassham, Gregory. "Lewis and Tolkien on the Power of the Imagination." In *C. S. Lewis as Philosopher: Truth, Goodness and Beauty*, edited by David Baggett et al., 245–60. Downers Grove: IVP Academic, 2008.
Barzun, Jacques. *The Use and Abuse of Art*. Princeton and Chichester: Princeton University Press, 1975.
Beauregard, Mario, and Denyse O'Leary. *The Spiritual Brain: A Neuroscientist's Case for the Existence of the Soul*. New York: HarperOne, 2007.
Berger, Peter. *A Rumor of Angels: Modern Society and the Rediscovery of the Supernatural*. New York: Doubleday, 1970.
Beversluis, John. *C. S. Lewis and the Search for Rational Religion*. Amherst, NY: Prometheus, 2007.
Camus, Albert. *Myth of Sisyphus and Other Essays*. New York: Vintage International, 1991.
Chesterton, G. K. *Orthodoxy*. Nashville: Sam Torode, 2009.
Connolly, Sean. *Inklings of Heaven: C. S. Lewis and Eschatology*. Gateshead: Athenaeum, 2007.
Copan, Paul. "The Naturalists Are Declaring the Glory of God." In *Philosophy and the Christian Worldview: Analysis, Assessment, and Development*, edited by Mark Linville and David Werther. New York: Continuum, 2012.
Copan, Paul, and William L. Craig, eds. *Contending with Christianity's Critics*. Nashville: B&H, 2009.
Craig, William Lane, and J. P. Moreland, eds. *The Blackwell Companion to Natural Theology*. Oxford: Wiley-Blackwell, 2009.
Crapps, Robert. *An Introduction to Psychology of Religion*. Macon, GA: Mercer University Press, 1986.
Dawkins, Richard. *The God Delusion*. Boston/New York: Houghton Mifflin, 2006.
Descartes, Rene. *Meditation on First Philosophy*, 4th ed. Indianapolis: Hackett, 1998.
Durkheim, Emile. *The Elementary Forms of Religious Life*. Translated by Carol Cosman. New York: Oxford University Press, 2008.

Bibliography

Eco, Umberto. *Art and Beauty in the Middle Ages.* New Haven/London: Yale University Press, 2002.

Ehrman, Bart. *God's Problem: How the Bible fails to Answer Our Most Important Question—Why We Suffer.* New York: HarperOne, 2008.

Esolen, Anthony. *Ten Ways to Destroy the Imagination of Your Child.* Wilmington, DE: Intercollegiate Institute, 2010.

Franken, Rombert. *Human Motivation.* 6th ed. Belmont, CA: Thomson Wadsworth, 2007.

Freud, Sigmund. *Civilization and Its Discontents.* New York: Norton, 2005.

———. *The Future of an Illusion.* New York: Norton, 1961.

Gerrig, Richard J., and Philip Zimbardo. *Psychology and Life,* 17th ed. New York: Pearson, 2005.

Holyer, Robert. "The Argument from Desire." *Faith and Philosophy* 5 (January 1988).

Husbands, Mark, et al., eds. *The Beauty of God: Theology and the Arts.* Downers Grove: IVP Academic, 2007.

Jacobs, Alan. "The Chronicles of Narnia." In *The Cambridge Companion to C. S. Lewis,* edited by Robert MacSwain and Michael Ward. New York: Cambridge University Press, 2010.

———. *The Narnian: The Life and Imagination of C. S. Lewis.* New York: HarperOne, 2006.

Kreeft, Peter. *Christianity for Modern Pagans: Pascal's Pensees.* San Francisco: Ignatius, 1993.

———. *Heaven: The Heart's Deepest Longing.* San Francisco: Ignatius, 1989.

———. "Lewis's Philosophy of Truth, Goodness and Beauty." In *C. S. Lewis as Philosopher: Truth, Goodness and Beauty,* edited by David Baggett et al., 245–60. Downers Grove: IVP Academic, 2008.

Kwan, Kai-Man. "The Argument from Religious Experience." In *The Blackwell Companion to Natural Theology,* edited by William Lane Craig and J. P. Moreland. Oxford: Wiley-Blackwell, 2009.

Lewis, C. S. *The Discarded Image: An Introduction to the Medieval and Renaissance Literature.* New York: Cambridge University Press, 2009.

———. *God in the Dock: Essays on Theology and Ethics,* edited by Walter Hooper. Grand Rapids: Eerdmans, 1970.

———. *The Great Divorce.* New York: HarperSanFrancisco, 2001.

———. *The Last Battle.* In *The Chronicles of Narnia in One Volume.* New York: HarperCollins, 2001.

———. *Letters to Malcolm: Chiefly on Prayer.* New York: Harcourt, 1992.

———. *The Magician's Nephew.* In *The Chronicles of Narnia in One Volume.* New York: HarperCollins, 2001.

———. *Mere Christianity.* New York: HarperSanFranciso, 2001.

———. *On Stories: And Other Essays on Literature.* Orlando: Harcourt, 1982.

———. *The Pilgrim's Regress: An Allegorical Apology for Christianity Reason and Romanticism.* Grand Rapids: Eerdmans, 1992.

———. *The Problem of Pain.* New York: Touchstone, 1996.

———. *Surprised by Joy.* Orlando: Harcourt, 1955.

———. *Till We Have Faces: A Myth Retold.* Orlando: Harcourt, 1984.

———. *Voyage of the Dawn Treader.* In *The Chronicles of Narnia in One Volume.* New York: HarperCollins, 2001.

———. *The Weight of Glory and Other Addresses.* New York: HarperOne, 2001.

Bibliography

Linville, Mark, and David Werther, eds. *Philosophy and the Christian Worldview: Analysis, Assessment, and Development.* New York: Continuum, 2012.

Lundin, Roger. *Believing Again: Doubt and Faith in a Secular Age.* Grand Rapids: Eerdmans, 2009.

———. "The Beauty of Belief." In *The Beauty of God: Theology and the Arts,* edited by Daniel Treier et al. Downers Grove: IVP Academic, 2007.

MacSwain, Robert, and Michael Ward, eds. *The Cambridge Companion to C. S. Lewis.* New York: Cambridge University Press, 2010.

Mayser, Sabine, et al. "(Un)Reachable?: An Empirical Differentiation of Goals and Life Longings." *European Psychologist* 13:2 (2008) 126–40.

McGrath, Alister. *Mere Apologetics: How to Help Seekers and Skeptics Find Faith.* Grand Rapids: Baker, 2012.

Midgley, Mary. *Beast and Man: The Roots of Human Nature.* London/New York: Routledge, 2006.

Murray, Michael. "Belief in God: A Trick of Our Brain?" In *Contending with Christianity's Critics,* edited by Paul Copan and William L. Craig. Nashville: B&H, 2009.

Nietzsche, Friedrich. *On the Genealogy of Morals.* Translated by Walter Kauffman. New York: Vintage, 1989.

Oakes, Edward T. "The Apologetics of Beauty." In *The Beauty of God: Theology and the Arts,* edited by Daniel Treier et al., 209–26. Downers Grove: IVP Academic, 2007.

Otto, Rudolf. *The Idea of the Holy.* Oxford: Oxford University Press, 1958.

Pascal, Blaise. *Pensees and Other Writings.* Oxford/New York: Oxford University Press, 2008.

Plantinga, Alvin. *Warrant and Proper Function.* New York/Oxford: Oxford University Press, 1993.

———. *Warranted Christian Belief.* New York/Oxford: Oxford University Press, 2000.

———. *Where the Conflict Really Lies: Science, Religion, & Naturalism.* New York/Oxford: Oxford University Press, 2011.

Plato. "Phaedo." In *Great Books of the Western World,* vol. 7, edited by Robert Maynard Hutchins. Chicago: Encyclopedia Britannica, 1952.

———. "Symposium." In *Great Books of the Western World,* vol. 7, edited by Robert Maynard Hutchins. Chicago: Encyclopedia Britannica, 1952.

Pieper, Josef. *Enthusiasm & Divine Madness: On the Platonic Dialogue Phaedrus.* South Bend: St. Augustine, 2000.

———. *Leisure: The Basis of Culture.* San Francisco: Ignatius, 2009.

Rahner, Karl. *Foundations of Christian Faith: An Introduction to the Idea of Christianity.* New York: Crossroad, 1978.

Reppert, Victor. *C. S. Lewis's Dangerous Idea: In Defense of the Argument from Reason.* Downers Grove: Intervarsity, 2003.

Roberts, W. Rhys. *Longinus On the Sublime: The Greek Text Edited After the Paris Manuscript,* translated by W. Rhys Roberts. 2d ed. New York: Cambridge University Press, 2011.

Scarry, Elaine. *On Beauty and Being Just.* Princeton: Princeton University Press, 1999.

Schaeffer, Francis. *How Should We Then Live: The Rise and Decline of Western Thought and Culture.* Wheaton, IL: Crossway, 2005.

Schall, James. *On the Unseriousness of Human Affairs.* Wilmington, DE: ISI, 2001.

———. *The Life of the Mind: On the Joys and Travails of Thinking.* Wilmington, DE: ISI, 2008.

Bibliography

Smith, Greg. "Pew Forum Survey on Religion in America." *Washington Post*, June 23, 2008.
Steiner, George. *Real Presences*. Chicago: University of Chicago Press, 1989.
Swinburne, Richard. *The Existence of God*. Oxford: Oxford University Press, 2004.
Taliaferro, Charles. "In Defense of the Numinous." In *Philosophy and the Christian Worldview*, edited by Mark Linville and David Werther. New York: Continuum, 2012.
Thayer, Joseph. *Thayer's Greek-English Lexicon of the New Testament*. Peabody, MA: Hendrickson, 1996.
Tolkien, J.R.R. *J.R.R. Tolkien: The Tolkien Reader*. New York: Ballantine, 1966.
Williams, Clifford. *Existential Reasons for Belief in God: A Defense of Desires and Emotions for Faith*. Downers Grove: IVP Academic, 2011.
Wright, N. T. *Simply Christian*. San Francisco: HarperSanFrancisco, 2006.

Subject/Name Index

1

1 Corinthians, 91
1 Peter, 146
1 Timothy, 67

A

a posteriori, 31-32, 49,54-55
a priori, 18, 31, 49, 54-55, 106
Acts, 62, 64, 68, 105
Adam, 101, 114, 147
Adams, Douglas, 87
Aesthetic, 16, 18, 22-23, 58-59, 64, 82, 98, 104-5, 107
afterlife, 17, 80, 124-25
agnostic, 6, 27, 64, 70, 72
Alper, Matthew, 80, 123-25, 127, 130, 137
annihilation, 121, 123, 125
Anselm, 145
anthropological, 9
anxiety, 8, 11, 58, 69
apologetics, 6, 45, 81, 85
apostle, 42, 64, 86, 91, 101
Aquinas, Thomas, 3, 29, 69, 84, 99, 102, 104-5, 135
Aristotle, 49-50, 100-2, 104, 113-14, 135-37
art, 23, 65, 82, 84, 98, 104, 106-9, 115
arts, 102-3, 107-9
Aslan, 33-34, 59-60, 115-17, 143-44
atheism, 4, 27, 54, 62-63, 66, 70, 72, 80, 83, 116, 125
Auden, W.H., 84, 105-7
Augustine, 12, 84, 146-47

B

baptism, 90, 106
Barzun, Jacques, 108-9
Bassham, Gregory, 90
Beauregard, Mario and O'Leary, Denyse, 125
beauty, 22, 40, 57, 64, 73, 76, 84-85, 87, 90-91, 98-110
behaviorists, 89
belief, 4, 6, 10-11, 20, 28-30, 32-34, 59, 80, 86, 105, 123-31, 133-34, 138
Belloc, Hilaire, 109
Berger, Peter, 18, 84
Bering, Jesse, 136-37
Beversluis, John, 37, 39, 41, 45-56, 59, 61-62, 64-68, 74, 76, 79, 123
Bible, 27, 29, 61-63, 65, 69, 84, 95, 111, 115
biological, 3, 23, 52-55, 126-27, 130, 134-35
Boethius, 84
brain, 4, 28-29, 46, 80, 93, 121, 124-25, 127-28, 134
Buddhism, 10

C

Calvin, John, 29
Carnell, Corbon Scott, 25
Cartesian (see also certainty and skepticism), 39, 106, 138
causation, 3, 25, 28, 51, 70, 74, 82, 91, 101, 103-5, 126, 129
certainty, 4, 8, 10-11, 25, 29-30, 35-39, 41, 51, 55-57, 62-64, 70, 76, 84, 93, 106-7, 114, 116, 128-29

Chesterton, G.K., 92–94, 97
Christ, 33, 42, 68, 109, 111
Christian, 5, 9, 12, 14–16, 39, 42, 54, 68, 85, 96, 100, 104, 147
Christianity, 10, 13–14, 19, 35–36, 39–41, 45, 68, 71, 75, 82–83, 86, 95
cognition, 4–5, 12, 29–32, 34, 68–69, 123–24, 131, 134–35, 138
Confucianism, 10
Connolly, Sean, 25
conscience, 3–5, 17, 28, 36, 67, 69–70, 73, 104, 130
Contemplation, 110, 112–13, 115, 117
Copan, Paul, 125–26, 130–32
cosmological argument, 3, 6, 141
cosmology, 104
cosmos, 3
Crapps, Robert, 9, 11
Creation, 10, 26, 53–54, 74, 84, 87, 93, 100–1, 108, 114–15, 117
creativity, 9–10, 12–13, 54, 94, 104, 114–15
Creator, 4, 29, 95, 100, 102–3, 130
creature, 10, 15, 17, 35, 39–40, 101, 104, 115–16
credulity, 131
cultural, 52, 72, 80–81, 84, 88, 90, 98, 104, 110, 112, 125
cultures, 10, 55, 125, 133–34
cumulative (case), 85, 141

D

Dante, 99, 102
Darwinian (see also evolution), 132
Dawkins, Richard, 86–87, 127–30
death, 9, 27, 38, 73, 80, 121, 123, 125, 127, 136, 148
deductive reasoning, 29, 35–39, 45, 48–50, 79, 83, 106
defeaters (undercutting and rebutting), 49, 123–25
Descartes, Rene, 30, 105–6
design, 3–5, 34, 53–55, 82–83, 135–36
desire, 5–16, 18–24, 27–28, 31–32, 35–42, 46–53, 55–59, 61–71, 74–75, 79–81, 84, 86, 95–96, 99–100, 104, 107, 109, 121, 123, 125–30, 132, 134
desires, 6, 9, 15–16, 19–20, 35, 37–41, 46–55, 68–69, 71, 74, 76, 79–80, 95, 98, 108, 121, 134, 141
deterministic, 130
disbelief, 74
discontentment, 11–12, 14, 22, 26, 113
disenchantment, of the world, 107
disposition, 29, 33, 71, 89, 134–36
divine, 3, 5–7, 9–10, 12, 16–18, 20, 24, 27, 29–30, 32, 41, 51, 54–55, 59–60, 65, 67–70, 74–75, 84–85, 90–91, 93, 95–102, 104–6, 109–10, 112, 115–17, 121, 127, 130, 132, 134–36
Donoghue, Denis, 98
dualism, 101, 106
Durkheim, Emile, 9–10

E

Earth, 12, 14, 20, 22–23, 27, 38, 40–42, 49, 57, 68, 79–81, 85, 87, 93, 95, 99–101, 103, 108–9, 115, 121, 136, 146–47
Ecclesiastes, 14–15, 63–64, 67, 100
echoes (of transcendence), 12, 32, 69, 74, 79, 81–85, 97–98, 110, 115, 139
education, 14–15, 62, 88
Ehrman, Bart, 70–71
emotion, 17, 22, 26, 30, 50, 59, 69–71, 82, 90, 98
empirical, 18, 49, 51, 54, 86–87, 91, 129
enchanted, 90
enlightenment, 103, 125
Epicurean, 64
erotic (desire), 20, 42
Esolen, Anthony, 88, 93
eternal, 7, 15, 23, 56, 67, 108–10, 123, 129
ethics, 114, 135–36
Eucatastrophe, 94, 96
Eudaimonia, 135–36
Eve, 101, 114, 147

evidence, 3, 10, 25, 28, 30, 34, 54–55, 62–63, 72, 81, 83, 85–86, 97, 105, 110, 129, 132–35, 137, 142
evolution (see also Darwinian), 4, 7, 9, 16, 26–34, 41, 46, 52–55, 80, 102, 121, 123, 125–34
existential, 5, 41, 54, 69
experiential, 55, 85

F

faculties (see also cognition), 4–5, 12, 29–34, 54–55, 68, 89, 93, 96, 131, 138
fairies, 15, 17, 83, 86–90, 93–97, 107
faith, 5–6, 12, 28–30, 39, 53, 69–71, 75–76, 90–91, 93, 104–5, 107, 109
Fall, the, 26, 29, 105
fantasy, 26, 89–90, 96
fear (eg., of death), 7–8, 12, 17–18, 33, 59–60, 68, 80, 115–16, 123, 125, 127
feelings, 6, 8, 10, 15–20, 22–27, 32, 35, 57–58, 64–65, 67–70, 73, 75–76, 82–83, 86, 89–90, 94, 100, 102–4, 106, 109, 111–12, 127, 141–42
finite, 3, 96, 102, 130
forgiveness, 70
Franken, Rombert, 114
freedom (eg., will), 31, 59, 68–69, 82, 108, 112, 130
Freud, Sigmund, 6–12, 18, 30, 86–87, 123, 127, 130, 137

G

Garden of Eden, 26, 57, 101, 114, 146–49
genes, 50, 55, 123, 133–34
Genesis, 29, 114, 147, 149
God, 3, 5–13, 15, 18, 20–21, 28–32, 34, 40, 42, 46, 48, 51–52, 54–56, 61–72, 74–76, 80, 83–86, 90–91, 93, 95–96, 98–99, 101–2, 104–16, 121, 123–25, 127, 129–30, 133–34, 136–38, 140, 145

good-catastrophe, 96
Gospel(s), 95, 97, 111
grace, 87, 94

H

Happiness, 11, 14, 22, 24, 36, 59, 64, 66–67, 73, 86–87, 89, 91, 93–97, 113, 135–36
Hardenberg, Friedrich von, 24
Haunted, 16–18, 62, 69, 77, 110, 113, 130
heart, 6, 11, 15, 23–24, 34, 56, 59, 61, 63, 73–76, 83, 86–87, 89, 91, 93, 95–97, 100, 112, 139–40
Heaven(s), 5–6, 12–14, 17, 20, 31, 36, 40, 42, 48, 59, 63, 66, 69, 74, 95–97, 100–1, 108, 113, 115, 121, 125, 130, 141
Hinduism, 10
Holyer, Robert, 18, 45, 47–48, 51, 79
Home, 7, 13, 19, 27, 42, 73, 76, 90, 117, 146
homesickness, 19, 26, 42, 147
hope, 19, 26, 59, 64, 68, 75, 109, 125
Hume, David, 106

I

idols, 87, 99–100, 108–9, 113
imagination, 7, 9–10, 26, 33, 36, 38, 51, 58, 74–75, 83–85, 87–90, 93, 95, 97–98, 107, 110, 129, 134, 148
incarnation, 95–96
inclination, 8–9, 30, 63, 72, 131
induction, 5, 18–19, 35, 38–39, 45, 48–49, 51, 79, 85
inherited (see also genes), 123, 133
innate, 9, 16, 28, 39–41, 48–55, 62, 66, 68, 74, 79–81, 84, 121, 124, 134, 136
instinct, 9, 16–17, 51–53, 68, 92, 96, 129
intuition, 65, 135, 139
Islam, 10

J

Jacobs, Alan, 24, 27, 145, 150
Jerusalem, 63
Jesus, 62, 64, 68, 91, 93–95, 101, 111, 145, 148, 150
Joy, 4, 6, 8, 10, 12–14, 16, 18–27, 30, 32, 34, 36–40, 42, 46–50, 52–76, 79–82, 84, 88, 90, 92, 94, 96, 100, 102, 104–6, 108, 110, 112–16, 121, 123–24, 126, 128, 130, 132–34, 136
Judaism, 10

K

Kreeft, Peter, 3, 5–6, 17, 36, 40, 42, 45, 48–50, 59, 66–68, 75, 83, 96, 98–99, 109, 113, 121, 142
Kwan, Kai-Man, 10, 72

L

Laughter, 49, 115–17
leisure, 84–85, 110–17
Lewis, C. S., 1, 4, 10, 12–41, 45–62, 65–67, 69, 71, 73–76, 79, 81–82, 84–88, 90–92, 95–97, 99–102, 104–5, 107–13, 115–17, 121, 123, 128, 132–36, 139–40, 142, 144, 146, 149–50
Linville, Mark, 85
Locke, John, 105
longing(s), 6–8, 12–16, 18–19, 23–27, 31–32, 34, 41–42, 46, 54, 56–60, 63–64, 67–68, 75–76, 81, 86, 88, 90, 96, 99, 108, 110, 112–13, 121, 123, 126, 128, 133, 141
Longinus, 82, 84
Lord's Supper, 147
love, 8, 19, 23, 58–59, 70, 76, 83–84, 87–88, 92, 100–1, 104, 109, 116
Lucy, 143–44
Lundin, Roger, 98–99, 107–8
Luther, Martin, 105–6

M

Malcolm, Leters to, 107, 112
materialist, 53, 62, 98
Matter, 101, 135
matter, 5–6, 29, 38–40, 63, 100–1, 106, 109, 127, 130, 135
Matthew, 62, 80, 93, 101, 111, 123, 148
Mayser, 25
McGrath, 5, 85
medieval, 102–4, 115
memory, 12, 29–30, 57, 99, 131, 147
messengers, 109
Midgley, 55, 89–90
Mill, 67
Milton, 57
mind, 4, 12, 14, 18, 20, 24, 28, 37, 60, 69, 88, 93–96, 99, 102–5, 111–13, 116, 130, 134 miracle, 33, 83, 89, 91–93, 117
morality, 3–4, 34, 59–60, 74, 82, 85, 98, 126
Murray, Michael, 133–39
mysterious, 14, 18, 20–21, 27, 31–33, 58, 66, 71, 80, 83, 93
mystical, 18, 28–29, 31, 33, 88
myth, 17, 87, 89, 96, 108

N

Narnia (Chronicles of), 13, 33, 59, 115, 117, 142, 145
naturalism, 4–5, 9, 90–91, 125–26, 130
needs, 8–9, 17–18, 20, 28, 53, 63, 69–71, 76, 95, 102, 110–11
neurological, 123
neuroscience, 134
Newtonian physics, 107
Nietzsche, Friedrich, 7, 9–10, 12, 16, 24, 137
noetic structure (see also cognition), 29
numinous (experiences), 16–18, 31, 33, 89, 95

O

oceanic feeling, 8
Omnipotence, 92, 140
Orual, 73–76
Otto, Rudolf, 16–18, 31, 33, 69, 79, 89, 95

P

Pascal, Blaise, 12, 68, 75, 83, 139–40, 142
Perelandra, 13
Philippians, 42, 111
Pieper, Josef, 110, 112–13, 149
Plantinga, Alvin, 4–5, 28–34, 69, 79, 131–32, 134
Plato, 12, 61, 84, 89, 99–2, 134, 147, 149
plausibility, 16, 38, 49–50, 121, 124, 126–28, 130, 132
play, as divine activity, 84, 87, 89–90, 92–93, 108, 110, 112–15, 117
Pleasure, 14–16, 18–19, 22–26, 35–36, 57, 64, 82, 104, 116
pornography, 100–1
Postmodernism, 99, 107
prayer, 49, 95, 110–12
predisposed, 30
preternatural, 96
probability, 15, 35–36, 35, 48, 126
Psyche, 72–73, 75–76
psychoanalytic, 7, 30
psychological, 3, 9, 12, 25, 41, 52–53, 70–71, 134
Puzzle, 59

R

Rahner, Karl, 30–31, 71, 79, 83
rationality, 4–6, 12, 27–30, 32–34, 38, 42, 51, 54, 83, 85–86, 104, 107, 131–32, 135–36
reality, 5, 10, 14, 16–18, 20, 30, 32–33, 36, 40, 48, 54, 68–69, 71, 73, 80–82, 84, 87–89, 91, 93, 95–98, 101, 104–6, 108, 116, 124–25, 128, 131–32 reason, 3–4, 24, 29–30, 36, 41, 48, 50–51, 53, 55, 58, 62–64, 72, 74, 83, 85, 90–91, 95, 101, 104, 107, 124, 126–27, 130–31, 133, 136, 140, 142
recollection, 89, 149
Reepicheep, 142–44
Reidian (common sense philosophy), 132
religion, 7–11, 16, 18, 72, 86, 104, 107, 125, 127, 137
religious, 6, 8, 10, 16, 95, 108, 125, 127–28, 134
remembering, 20, 57, 65, 75, 85, 134, 146–49
Reppert, Victor, 4, 85
Revelation, 149
revelation, 18, 27, 29, 84, 104
Romans, 26, 65, 101, 150

S

Scarry, Elaine, 98–99
Schaeffer, Francis, 104
Schall, James, 111, 114
Schleiermacher, Friedrich, 16
scientism, 88
scientist, 28, 88, 90–91, 107, 109, 121, 134
secular, 53, 63, 88, 90, 109
Sehnsucht (i.e., Joy), 22–29, 31–34, 41–42, 52–53, 55, 58, 61, 63–65, 67, 69, 75, 79, 81, 100, 108, 110–11, 113, 115, 117, 133, 135–36, 138–40, 142, 146–47, 149–50
sensus divinitatis, 29, 32–33, 69, 105
sex, 6, 15, 35, 40–41, 51, 84, 92, 101
sexual (see also desire), 15, 35
shadows, 17, 96, 100
signal(s), 18, 84, 90, 101
signs (eg., of transcendence), 74, 80, 82, 85, 106
Sikhism, 10
sin, 26, 29, 74, 101, 116–17
skeptic(s), 86, 88, 99, 116
skepticism, 33, 51, 88, 91, 93, 98, 102, 106, 115
Socrates, 50, 67, 99
solipsism, 28

spirit(s), 20, 26, 29, 39, 72, 95, 108, 113, 123
spiritual, 9, 12, 30, 53, 72, 80, 82, 90, 107, 112, 123–25, 134
St. John, 37, 41, 45, 52, 67, 79, 86, 91, 105, 123
St. Luke, 111, 117
St. Mark, 85, 111
St. Paul, 26, 42, 62, 64–65, 67–69, 91, 101, 111, 125, 148
Steiner, George, 81–82, 109
Stoicism, 64
subconscious, 7, 18
subjective, 3, 5, 17, 36, 79, 99, 106–7
sublime, 12, 82–84
suffering, 58, 71, 83, 116
supernatural, 7, 42, 51, 53, 65, 91–92, 94, 96, 129, 131–32, 136, 140
Swinburne, Richard, 126, 131–32

T

Taliaferro, Charles, 10, 72–73, 124
teleological, 3, 6, 135
teleology, 107, 135
telos, 54, 135–36
testimony, 28, 131
theism, 4–5, 9–10, 29, 121, 124–26, 129–31, 135
Thomist (see also Aquinas), 49–50
Tirian, 59–60
Tolkien, J.R.R., 90, 94–97
tradition, 9–10, 49–50, 128, 134, 148
transcendence, 3, 5, 7, 9–12, 18–20, 31, 46, 51, 57–58, 62, 64–65, 68–69, 76, 80–82, 84–85, 88, 95–97, 100–6, 109–10, 113, 115, 121, 123, 126, 128–32, 134
transcendental, 71, 81
transport, 82, 84

U

Uncle Andrew, 33–34, 115–17
urgings, 67
utilitarian, 84, 114

V

virtue, 11, 111, 136

W

wager, 81–82
warrant, 4, 6, 28–29, 32, 34, 39, 45, 51, 125, 138
Williams, Clifford, 69–70, 76, 139
wonder, 17, 32, 47, 50, 52, 56, 61, 82–84, 90, 92–93, 96, 99, 102–5
workday, 112, 114
worldview, 12, 54, 90, 100, 102
worship, 9, 17, 64, 81, 87, 96, 109, 134
Wright, N.T., 9, 12

Y

yearning(s), 24, 58, 149

Z

Zeus, 65

www.ingramcontent.com/pod-product-compliance
Lightning Source LLC
Chambersburg PA
CBHW070922180426
43192CB00038B/2163